400
Smokin' Bluegrass
Banjo Licks

by Eddie Collins

ISBN 978-1-57424-298-0
SAN 683-8022

Cover by James Creative Group

Cover illustration by Kevin Delaney

Copyright © 2013 CENTERSTREAM Publishing, LLC
P.O. Box 17878 - Anaheim Hills, CA 92817

www.centerstream-usa.com

TABLE OF CONTENTS & TRACK LIST

TABLE OF CONTENTS & TRACK LIST (CONTINUED)

BOOK OVERVIEW

This book is designed to to help you improvise bluegrass style banjo solos based on licks played over given chord progressions. In this style of soloing, the use of licks may take precedent over stating the melody. While the licks may be inserted into both vocal tunes and fiddle tunes, the progressions used are based primarily on common vocal numbers.

LEVEL OF DIFFICULTY

The content of this book is considered to be at an intermediate level and beyond. You should already be familiar with standard Scruggs style and be familiar with the concepts of *single-string* (Reno) and *melodic* (Keith) styles. You should know left-hand techniques, such as slides, hammer-ons and pull-offs, and be familiar with naming chords as numbers, such as I, IV and V.

TUNING THE BANJO • TAB

Only standard G tuning is used throughout this book: G, D, G, B, D (strings 5 through 1). Tune to an electronic tuner and you will be in tune to the CD tracks.

The music in this book is presented in a notation system called *tablature* ("tab" for short). Five parallel lines placed horizontally represent each of the five strings, not the traditional music staff. In this system, the 1st string is placed on top, instead of on the bottom the way it is normally viewed. The drawing below demonstrates how the five lines of tablature translate to the five strings of the banjo. A number on a line equals the fret to be played on that string. Left-hand fingers are referred to as 1 – 4 (Index through Pinky). Right-hand fingers are identified as T, I and M (Thumb, Index and Middle). A complete Tablature Guide is given on page 66.

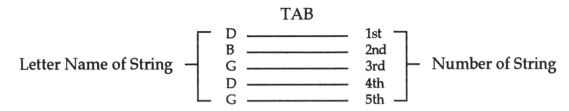

Only tablature has been used, instead of combining it with musical notation, to allow the maximum amount of information to be conveyed in the least amount of space. All of the licks are in 4/4 "common" time.

THE PRACTICE CD

All of the licks are presented at a learning speed. There is a separate guitar accompaniment when a complete solo is performed. The banjo melody and rhythm guitar tracks are recorded separately. Turn the balance control right to hear mostly melody (to learn a song), or left to hear mostly rhythm (to practice performing a piece). A CD symbol informs you where to locate a lick or song on the CD. If you need the song slowed down for practice, try acquiring software that can digitally slow down the track without altering it's pitch.

TAG LICKS – KEY OF G

Tag licks are those that are added as a conclusion to a solo, or the phrase that is added to fill the space during a pause in the vocal phrasing. Lick #1 is a variant of the most common lick Earl Scruggs used for this purpose. Basic tag licks simply take up one measure followed by a measure of rest, or readjusting to return to rhythm. All the licks below can serve the same function even as they become quite elaborate.

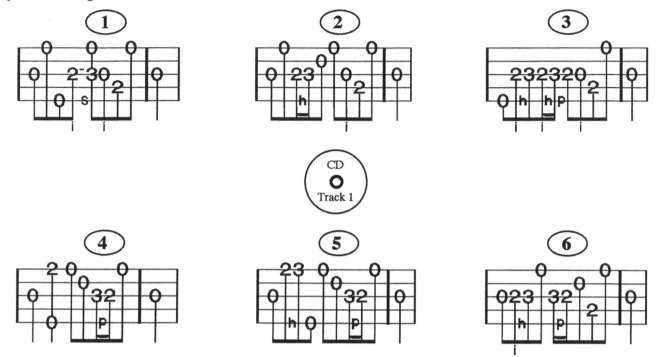

D LICKS

D is the most common chord in the measure preceding a final G tag lick. We are basically building a solo from the end. Many D licks are built off D7 like #s 7 and 8 below.

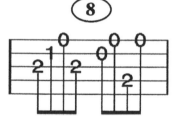
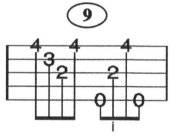

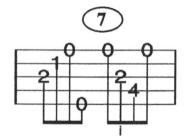
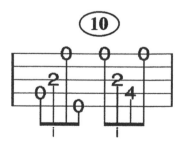
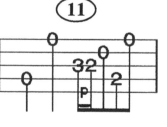
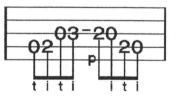

G LICKS

Technically, the tag licks on page 5 could be considered G licks, as they are played over a background G chord. However, tags licks have a certain conclusive sound about them that lends them inappropriate in certain contexts. The G licks below are much more universal.

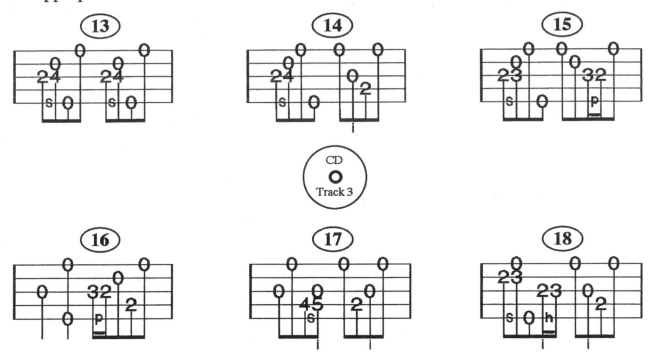

REUSING IDEAS • FORMING PHRASES

Many D licks can also be used as G licks. The criteria is simply that the notes sound plausible against the given background chord. D licks #s 11 and 12 could also be used as G licks as they contain enough notes from a G chord to make them sound good in that context.

Let's now try a couple of combinations of licks that could serve as the last phrase to any solo ending G D G G.

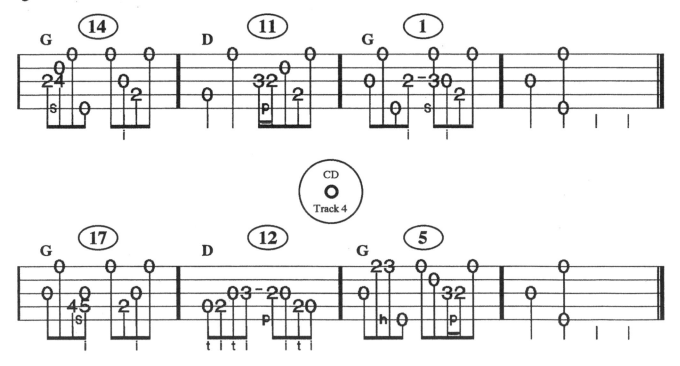

LEAD-INS

Lead-in licks are often played to begin a song or solo and are less than a measure in length. Lead-ins in the key of G tend to resolve to a note within the G chord. The licks below resolve to the pitch equal of one of the open strings. Many of these sounds should be familiar.

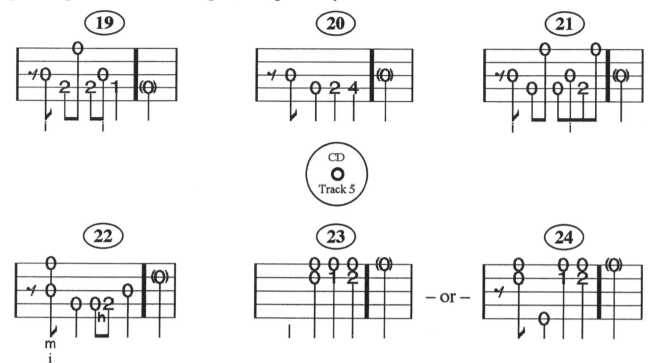

TURNAROUND INTRODUCTIONS

Vocal songs often begin with a short instrumental phrase. As we saw on page 6, the last phrase to many songs is played over G D G G. Sometimes the instrumentalist begins by playing the exact notes the singer would sing during the final phrase. Other times, he/she would play a generic all-purpose phrase such as the two below, which begin with lead-ins, play G and D licks and conclude with a Tag lick These phrases could be thought of as I V I intros.

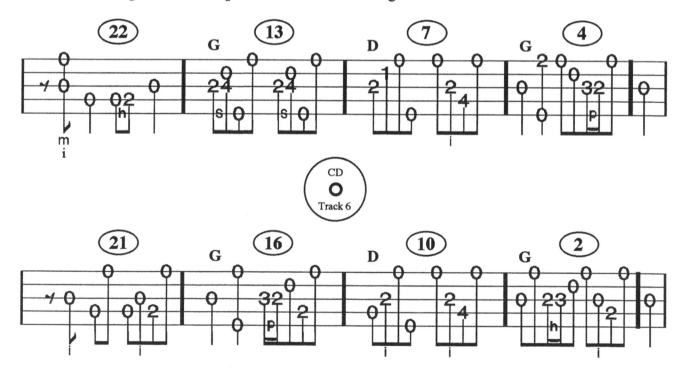

7

TWO-MEASURE G LICKS

Progressions often stay on the same chord for more than one measure. Here, you can think of two measures as a combination of two of your one-measure licks, or as a single two-measure lick where both measures are needed to complete the musical thought.

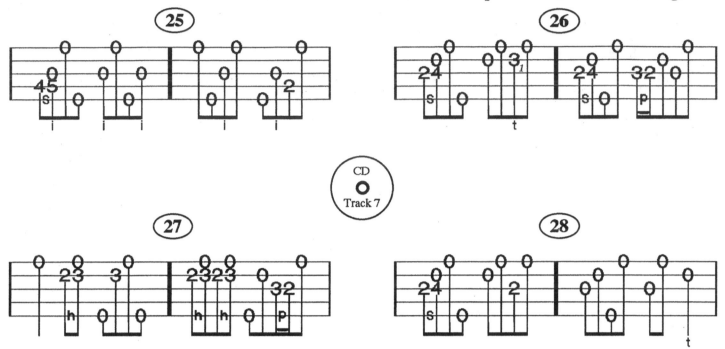

TWO-MEASURE D LICKS

As the name implies, two-measure D licks are those that fill two measures of D.

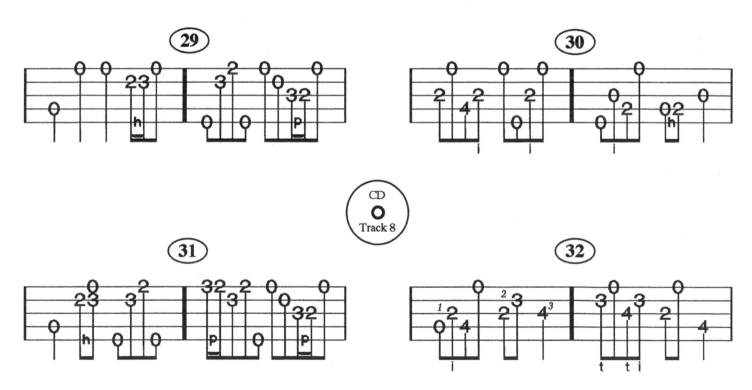

8

PLAYING OVER CHORD PROGRESSIONS

The following solos play over a specific repeating group of chords – a *progression*. Common progressions form the basis for hundreds of tunes, so learning to solo over them prepares you to solo over numerous traditional bluegrass songs. Progression #1 forms the foundation for songs such as "Blue Ridge Mountain Blues" and "Jambalaya."

Note: You normally play through an eight-measure progression twice per lead.

Chord Progression #1

G | G | D | D |
D | D | G | G ||

Chord Progression #1 – Solo 1

Chord Progression #1 – Solo 2

BLUE NOTE LICKS

Many bluegrass banjo licks sound bluesy. This sound can be created by adding *blue* notes–the *flatted 3rd* and *7th* notes from the key. Although there are others, these notes–Bb and F–are the most common blue notes in bluegrass. The flatted 3rd is often immediately followed by the major 3rd.

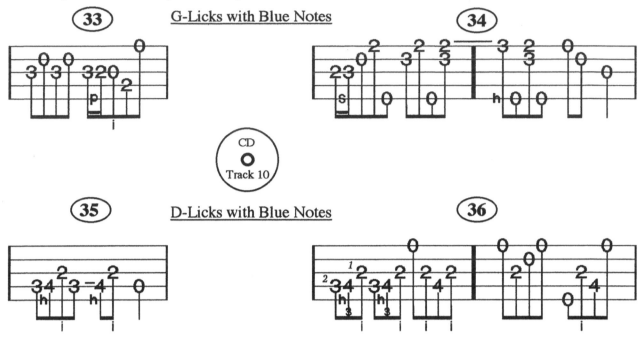

LICKS WITH PICK-UP NOTES

Sometimes thought of as *anticipatory* notes, pick-up notes start on a beat other than 1 leading to the strong downbeat of the lick on beat 1. Unlike the lead-in phrases we previously saw (page 8), pick-up notes do not stand as a lick unto themselves, but rather are the beginning notes of a complete phrase and often begin on beat 4.

CHORD PROGRESSION #2

This new progression will provide you with another chance to practice using all the types of G and D licks we have studied so far. Progression #2 is the series of chords used in songs such as "Handsome Molly" and "Tom Dooley."

Chord Progression #2

CD O Track 12

G | G | G | D |
D | D | D | G ||

Chord Progression #2 – Solo 1

Chord Progression #2 – Solo 2

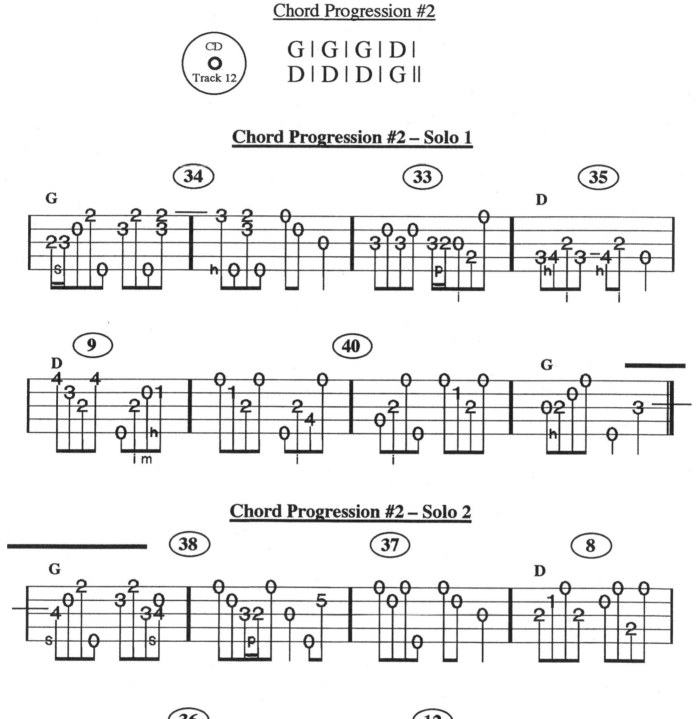

C LICKS

The next most common chord in the key of G beyond G (I) and D (V) is C, the IV chord. C licks come in all the same forms and lengths that we have studied thus far.

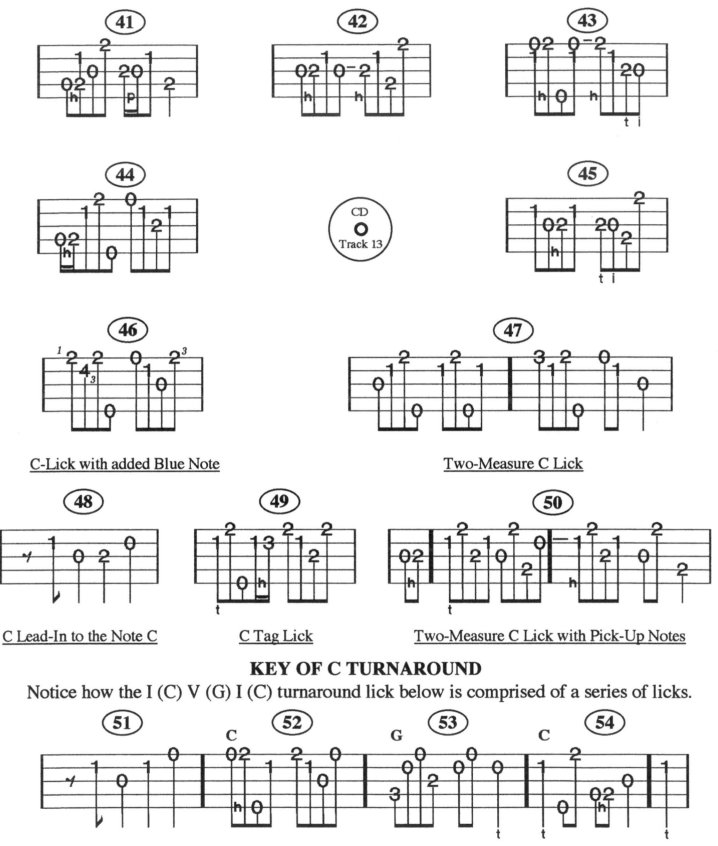

C-Lick with added Blue Note

Two-Measure C Lick

C Lead-In to the Note C

C Tag Lick

Two-Measure C Lick with Pick-Up Notes

KEY OF C TURNAROUND

Notice how the I (C) V (G) I (C) turnaround lick below is comprised of a series of licks.

C Lead-In to the Note E

C Lick

G Lick

C Tag Lick

CHORD PROGRESSION #3

The progression that follows includes G, C and D licks. It could be used for songs such as "Great Speckled Bird" and a whole series of tunes in the *talking blues* tradition, such as "Smoke That Cigarette."

Chord Progression #3

CD
O
Track 14

G | G | C | C |
D | D | G | G ||

Chord Progression #3 – Solo 1

Chord Progression #3 – Solo 2

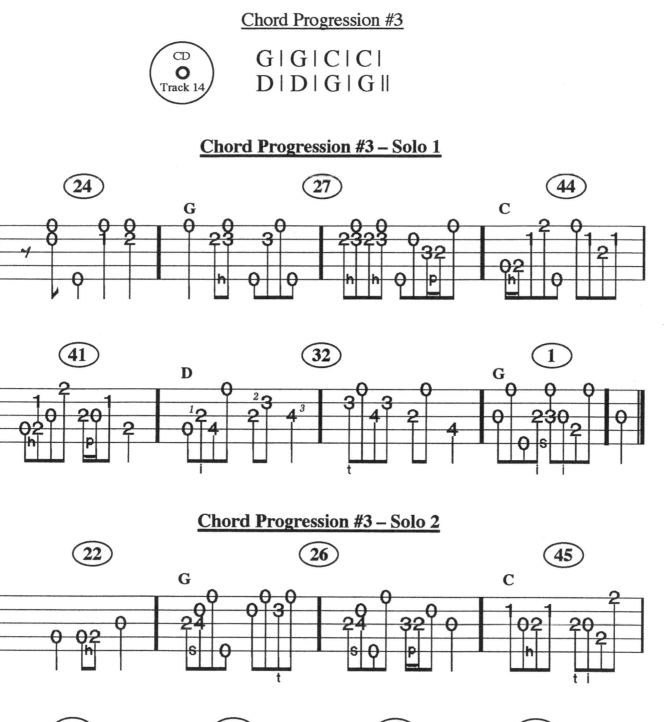

FRETTED EQUIVALENTS

It is very common for bluegrass banjo players to fret a note that is equivalent to doubling the sound of an open string. For example, lick #13 on page 6 uses a common 2 - 4 slide, with the 4th fret on string 3 being the same pitch as the open 2nd string. You thus have a choice to play either, or both notes to get the desired sound.

PENTATONIC SCALES

A Major *pentatonic* scale is made up of five notes – the 1st, 2nd, 3rd, 5th and 6th notes of a Major scale, omitting the 4th and 7th. Many of the licks we have learned have contained only notes from the pentatonic scale, i.e #s 32 and 44. Below are the first-position pentatonic notes available for G, C and D and a lick derived from each.

Note: The roots of each scale are circled. Fretted equivalents are in parentheses.

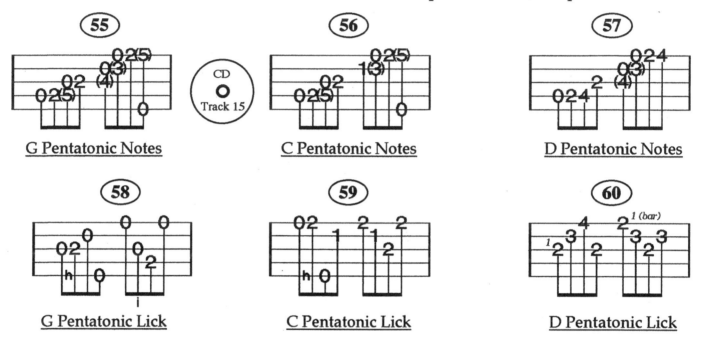

G Pentatonic Notes   C Pentatonic Notes   D Pentatonic Notes

G Pentatonic Lick   C Pentatonic Lick   D Pentatonic Lick

IMPROVISING A SOLO USING PENTATONIC SCALES

Pentatonic scales work great for creating a solo on the fly as they contain what can be considered *safe* notes – ones likely not to create much dissonance. Rather than totally winging it, your improvising may sound better when using these guidelines:

- Select notes from the Major pentatonic scale of the background chord.
- The open 5th string is in the G and C pentatonic scales, but not D.
- Think of your ideas as chord tones plus added safe notes.
- Any sustained note should be a note of the background chord.

An improvised solo is one where not every note is worked out ahead of time. As such, the solo on page 15 is merely an example of how a solo using pentatonic scales might sound. The scale tones for now are only from the first position. Notes from each pentatonic scale can be found all over the neck, so eventually you'd want to learn to apply the concept in other positions.

CHORD PROGRESSION #4

Here we have the most common progression in all of bluegrass. Tunes like "Your Love Is Like A Flower" and "Bury Me Beneath The Willow" utilize it. Solo 1 is based on licks and phrases derived from the pentatonic scale of the background chord.

Note: Licks not previously presented are given a new ID number.

Chord Progression #4

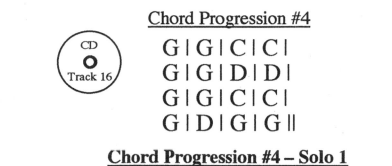

G | G | C | C |
G | G | D | D |
G | G | C | C |
G | D | G | G ‖

Chord Progression #4 – Solo 1

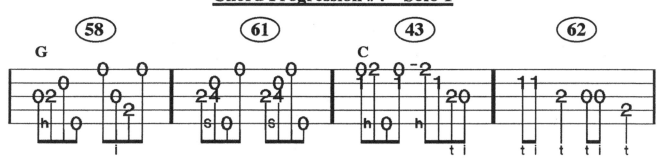

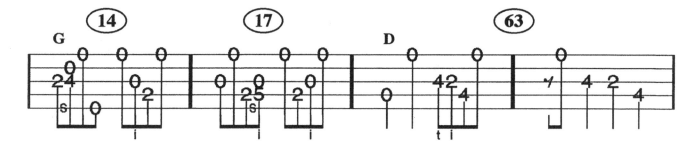

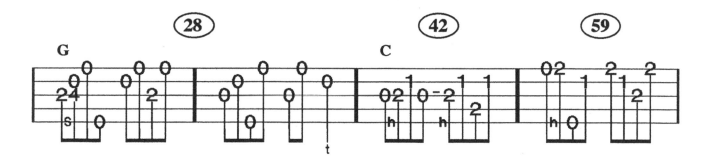

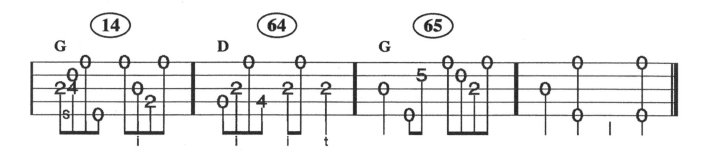

MODIFYING LICKS

Although not noted, there have been times in the solos where a couple of notes of a lick were changed to make the transition to the next phrase smoother.

CONNECTING RUNS

Connecting runs are those that lead the listener from one phrase to the next, especially when changing chords. They are like lead-ins where the expectation is that of a specific note after the run. They are different in that they will be complete measures

G to C Run

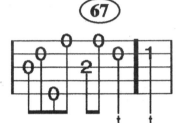

Another G to C Run

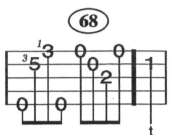

G to C with Flatted 7th

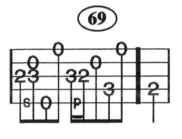

G to the Note E of C Chord

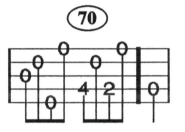

G to D Run

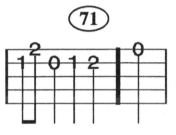

C to D Run

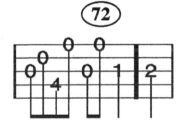

G to the Note A of D Chord

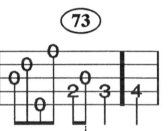

G to the Note F# of D Chord

V V I Turnaround With Connecting Run

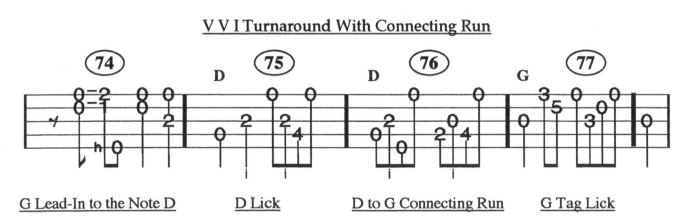

G Lead-In to the Note D   D Lick   D to G Connecting Run   G Tag Lick

CHORD PROGRESSION #4 – SOLO 2

Let's construct another solo over the chord changes we were introduced to on page 15. Instead of only using notes from the pentatonic scales, we'll open up the play book to include all of the families of licks we've studied and include connecting runs.

Note: Licks not previously presented are given a new ID number.

Chord Progression #4

G	G	C	C
G	G	D	D
G	G	C	C
G	D	G	G ‖

CD O Track 18

Chord Progression #4 – Solo 2

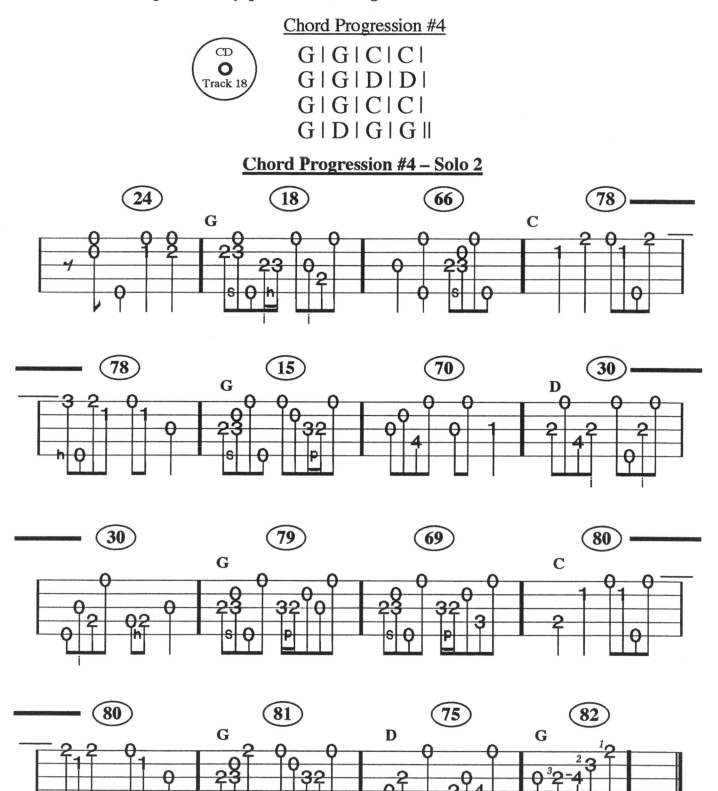

RENO STYLE LICKS

Don Reno incorporated both the use of licks that included a lot of guitar-like alternate Thumb/Index picking and triplets. Below are some similar to what he would play.

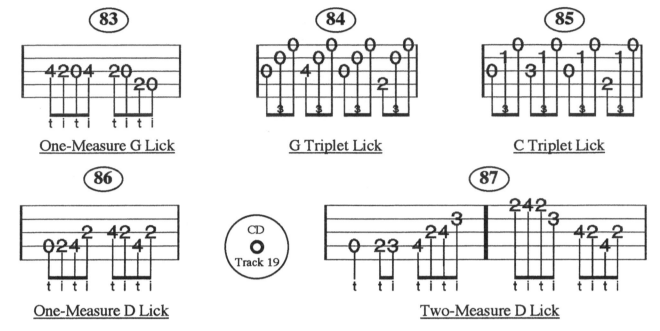

One-Measure G Lick   G Triplet Lick   C Triplet Lick

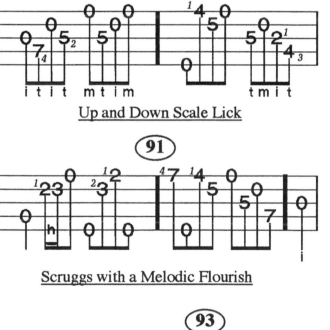

One-Measure D Lick   Two-Measure D Lick

MELODIC STYLE LICKS

Melodic style avoids striking the same string on consecutive 8th notes. Though the feeling is similar, you won't be playing rolls. Playing frets 4 - 7 is common in the style.

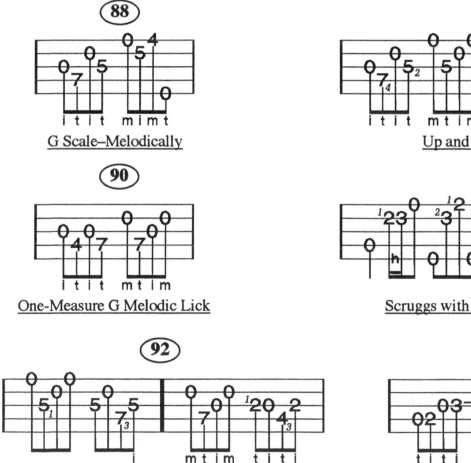

G Scale–Melodically   Up and Down Scale Lick

One-Measure G Melodic Lick   Scruggs with a Melodic Flourish

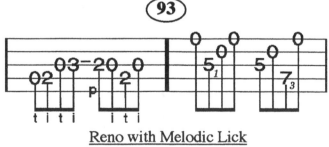

Melodic with Reno Lick   Reno with Melodic Lick

CHORD PROGRESSION #5

The chorus of many songs, including "Way Downtown" and even "Dueling Banjos" begin on the IV chord and follow the structure of Progression #5. Here you are given the chance to practice your Reno and Melodic licks. New licks will get new ID numbers.

Chord Progression #5

C | C | G | G |
D | D | G | G ||

CD Track 20

Chord Progression #5 – Solo 1

Chord Progression #5 – Solo 2

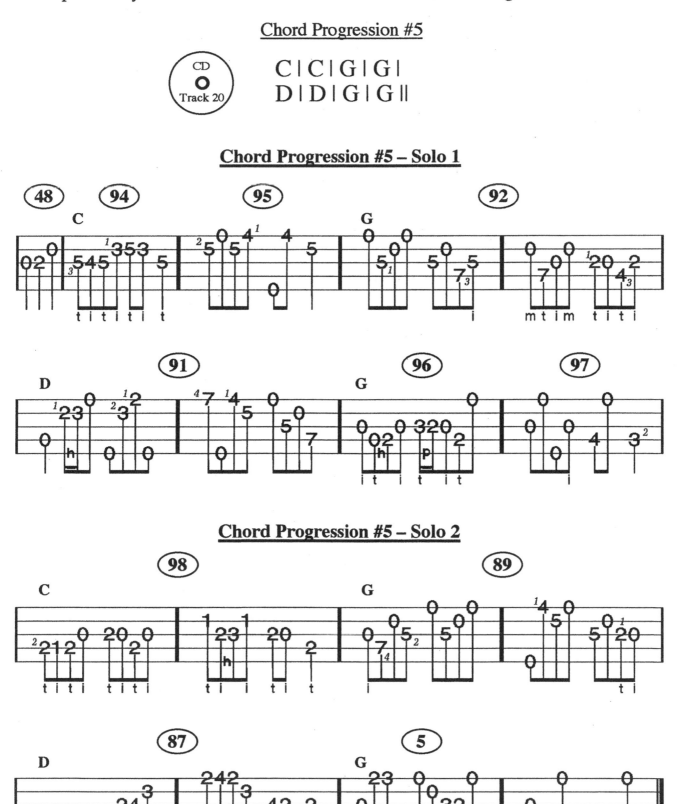

19

PENTATONIC BLUES SCALE

A five-note blues scale contains the flatted 3rd and flatted 7th of the key. It is sometimes called the G Minor Blues scale, but also plays over Major and modal chord changes. The notes in parentheses are the fretted equivalents of an open string.

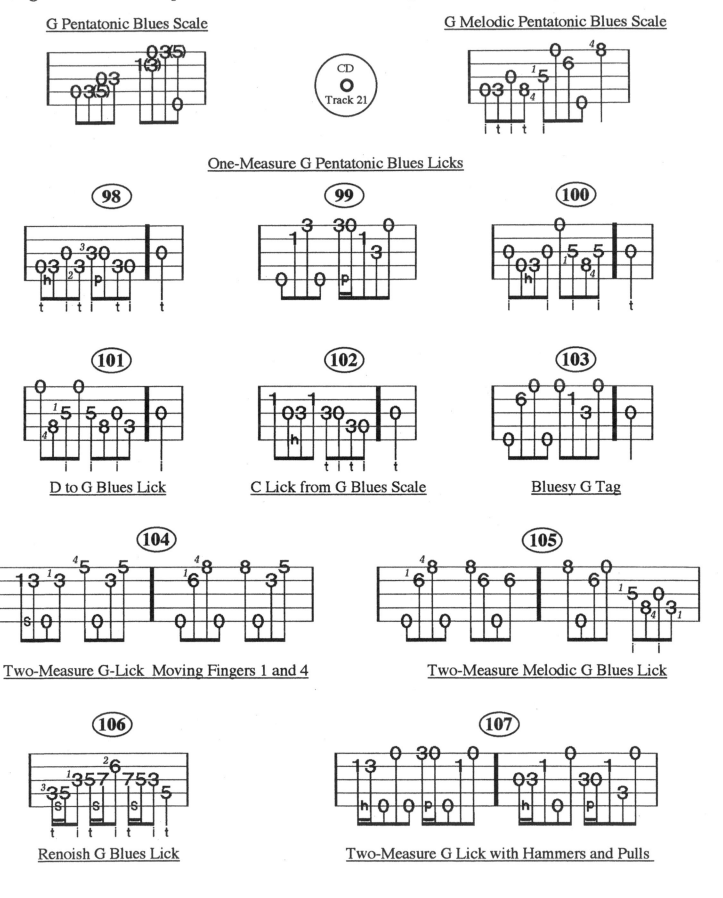

G Pentatonic Blues Scale

G Melodic Pentatonic Blues Scale

One-Measure G Pentatonic Blues Licks

98

99

100

101

102

103

D to G Blues Lick

C Lick from G Blues Scale

Bluesy G Tag

104

105

Two-Measure G-Lick Moving Fingers 1 and 4

Two-Measure Melodic G Blues Lick

106

107

Renoish G Blues Lick

Two-Measure G Lick with Hammers and Pulls

CHORD PROGRESSION #6

This new progression forms the basis for tunes such as "Wild Bill Jones" and "Train 45." Each pass through utilizes ideas from the pentatonic blues scale and includes many of the licks from page 20. New licks will get new ID numbers.

Chord Progression #6

CD
O
Track 22

G | G | G | G |
G | D | G | G ||

Chord Progression #6 – Solo 1

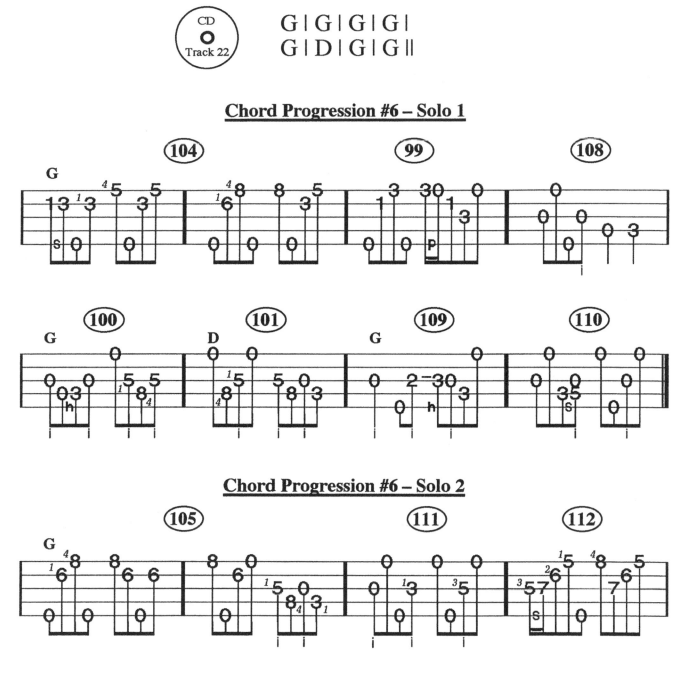

Chord Progression #6 – Solo 2

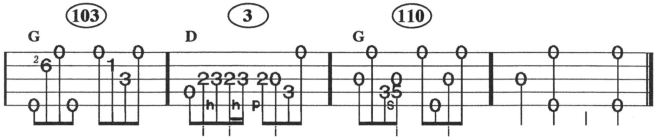

BOOGIE LICKS

Boogie woogie licks usually mimic the left hand of pianists playing in the style. One-measure phrases can be expanded into two-measure licks. Reno's and Eddie Adcock's influence is evident here. Flatted 3rds and 7ths are common in such licks.

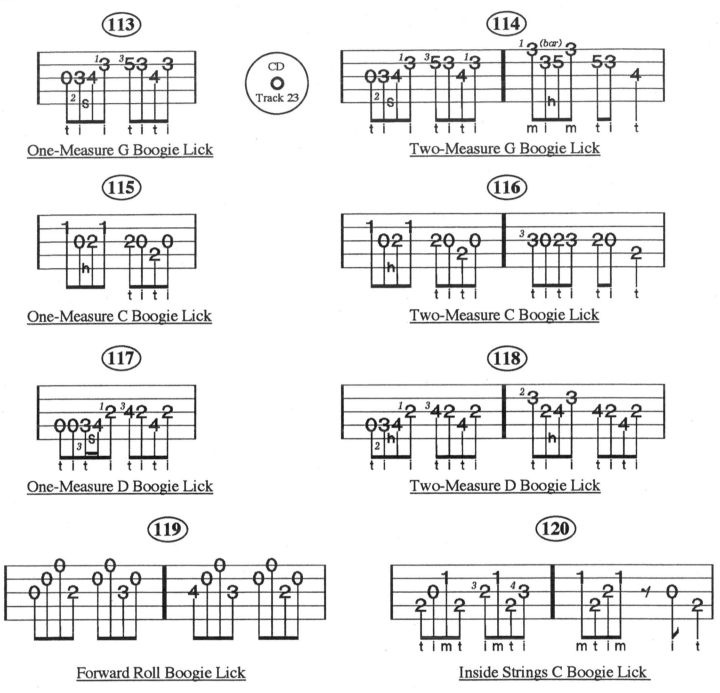

One-Measure G Boogie Lick

Two-Measure G Boogie Lick

One-Measure C Boogie Lick

Two-Measure C Boogie Lick

One-Measure D Boogie Lick

Two-Measure D Boogie Lick

Forward Roll Boogie Lick

Inside Strings C Boogie Lick

12 BAR BLUES

A 12 bar blues in bluegrass usually takes the form of Progression #7. Tunes like "Foggy Mountain Special" and Hank Williams' "Mind Your Own Business" follow it.

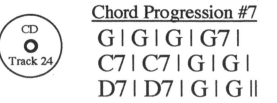

<u>Chord Progression #7</u>
G | G | G | G7 |
C7 | C7 | G | G |
D7 | D7 | G | G ||

22

Chord Progression #7 – Solo 1

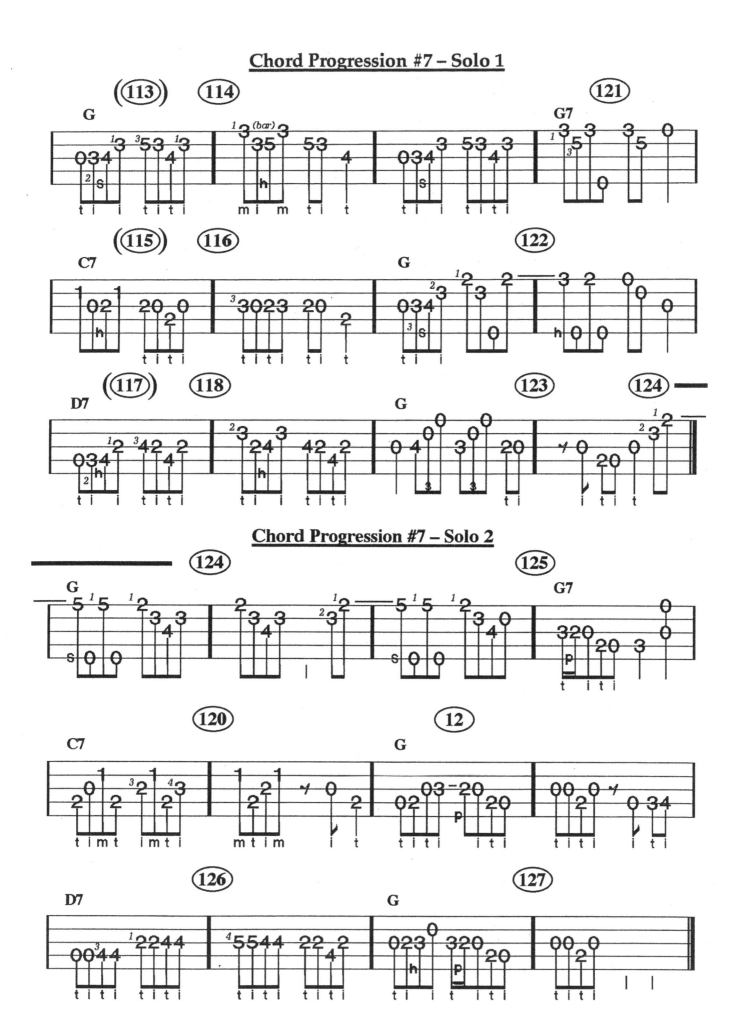

Chord Progression #7 – Solo 2

SWING PHRASING

Bill Monroe and Earl Scruggs were developing their music in the 1930s and 40s when swing was popular. We saw our first swing phrases, which often begin and/or end on the *and* of the beat in the solos on page 23. Another swing feature is a repeated series of three notes that create different syncopations (#s 128 and 129).

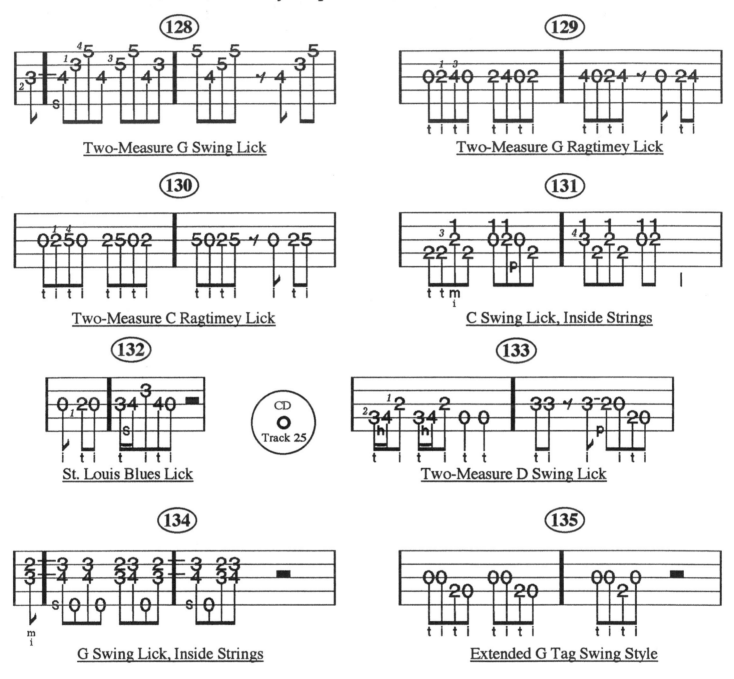

Two-Measure G Swing Lick

Two-Measure G Ragtimey Lick

Two-Measure C Ragtimey Lick

C Swing Lick, Inside Strings

St. Louis Blues Lick

Two-Measure D Swing Lick

G Swing Lick, Inside Strings

Extended G Tag Swing Style

MORE 12 BAR BLUES

Let's take another pass at Progression #7 (page 22). We'll add swing phrases and also licks from our earlier studies. As before, new licks will receive a new ID number.

Chord Progression #7 – Solo 3

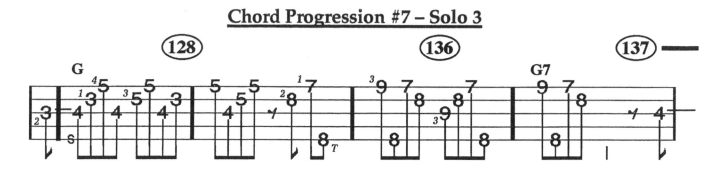

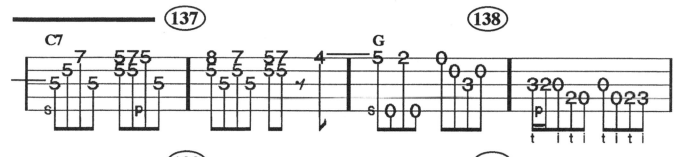

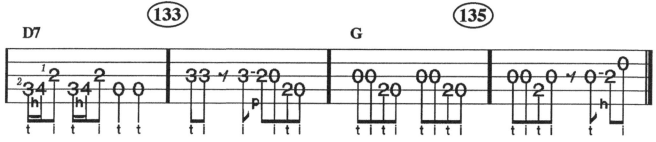

Chord Progression #7 – Solo 4

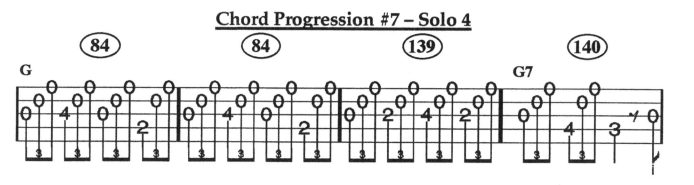

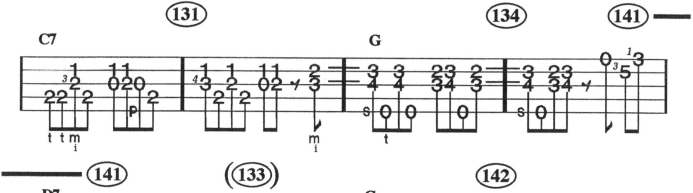

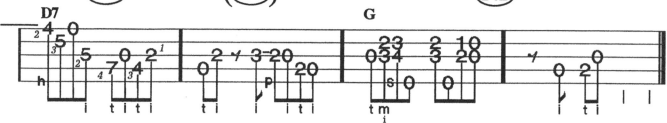

SEQUENTIAL LICKS

Licks that repeat a melodic idea can be viewed as a sequence of notes. A sequence can be a repeated idea of scale tones (#s143 - 145), moving a chord shape with a roll (#s146 - 148), or a series of intervals, such as 3rds (#149).

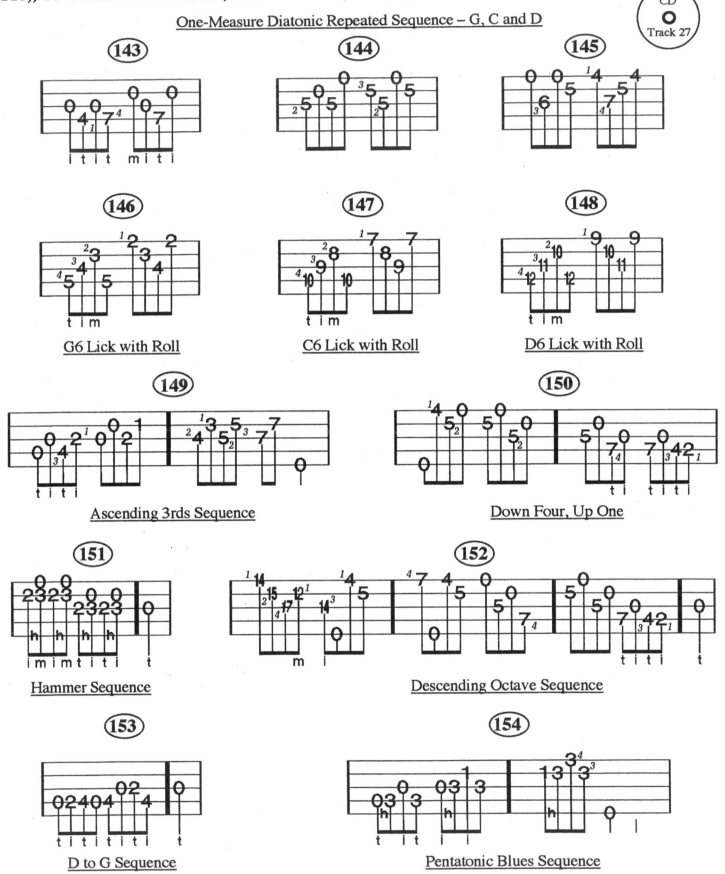

One-Measure Diatonic Repeated Sequence – G, C and D

CD
O
Track 27

G6 Lick with Roll

C6 Lick with Roll

D6 Lick with Roll

Ascending 3rds Sequence

Down Four, Up One

Hammer Sequence

Descending Octave Sequence

D to G Sequence

Pentatonic Blues Sequence

CHORD PROGRESSION #8

Part B of several fiddle tunes, such as "Big Sandy" and "Banjo Signal" use the following progression. The quick one-measure changes make it perfect for the use of sequential licks. New licks get new ID numbers.

Chord Progression #8

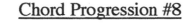

G | C | D | G |
G | C | D | G ‖

Track 28

Chord Progression #8 – Solo 1

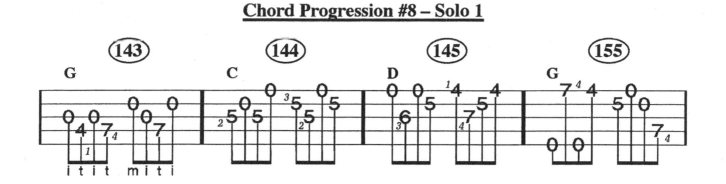

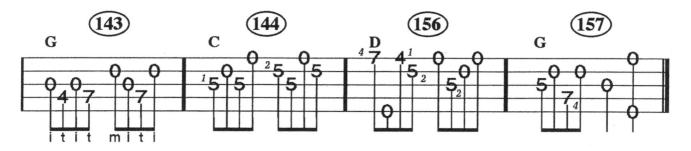

Chord Progression #8 – Solo 2

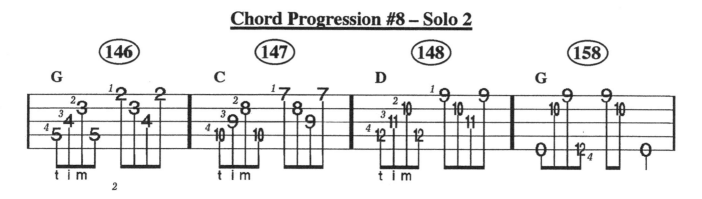

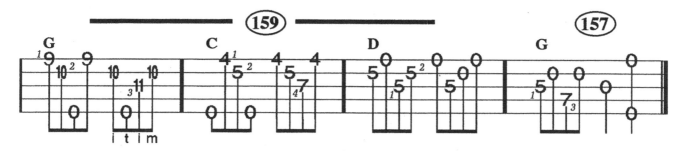

27

FOUR MEASURES OF G

Many progressions, like numbers 6 and 7, begin with four measures of G – the I chord. Ideas for such licks include repeating a motif before transitioning in the last measure (#160), establishing a sequence of slurs (#162), developing a diatonic or chromatic sequence (#163), or playing an interesting roll off a series of chord shapes (#164).

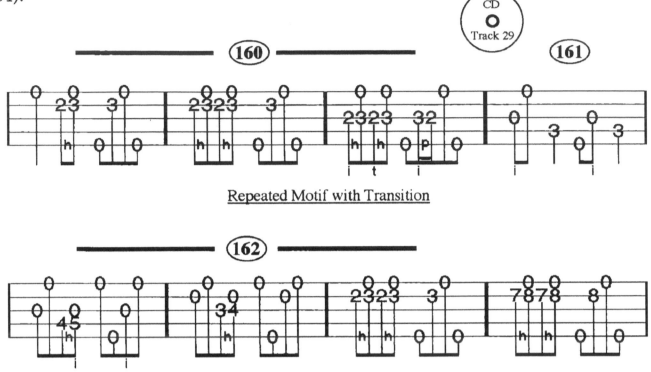

Repeated Motif with Transition

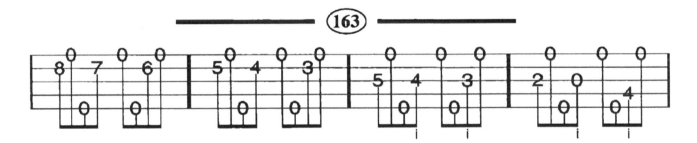

A Sequence of Hammer-Ons

A Descending Chromatic Run

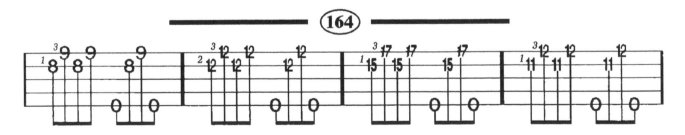

Playing Off Partial Chord Shapes

CHORD PROGRESSION #9

The following progression is used for many vocal songs, including "Circle Be Unbroken," "Mountain Dew" and "Sitting On Top Of The World." Begin with a four-measure G lick with the last measure transitioning to C. Again, licks not previously presented are given a new ID number.

Chord Progression #9

G | G | G | G |
C | C | G | G |
G | G | G | G |
G | D | G | G ‖

Chord Progression #9 – Solo 1

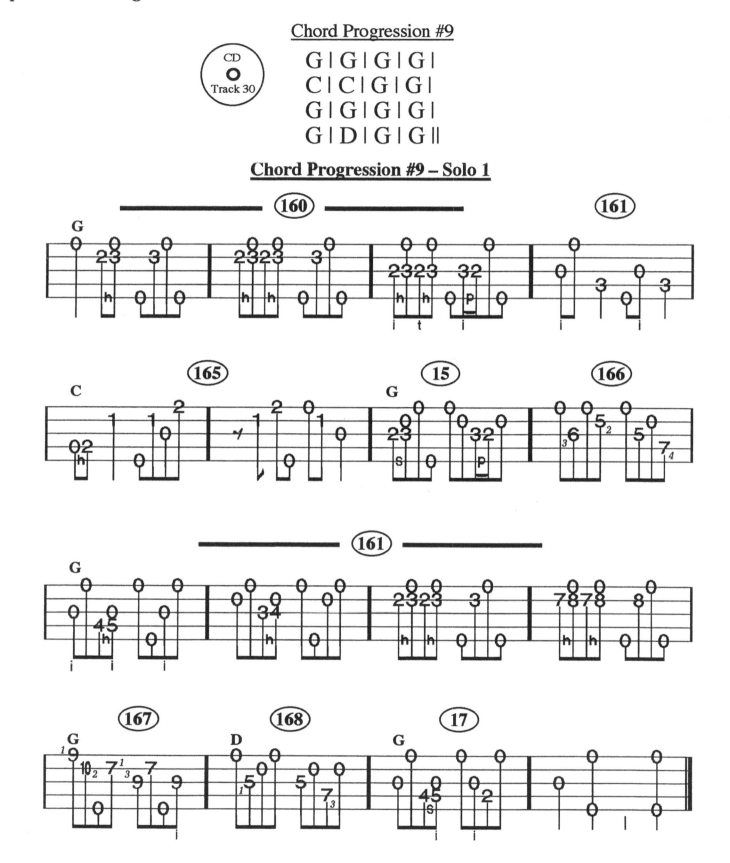

BACK-UP LICKS

Back-up licks can generally be thought of as serving two functions. They can help drive the rhythm through the use of chord vamps (#169) or extended rolls (#170). Back-up licks may also come in the form of musical statements that fill the holes between vocal phrases (#s 171 and 172). Some licks are used for both purposes.

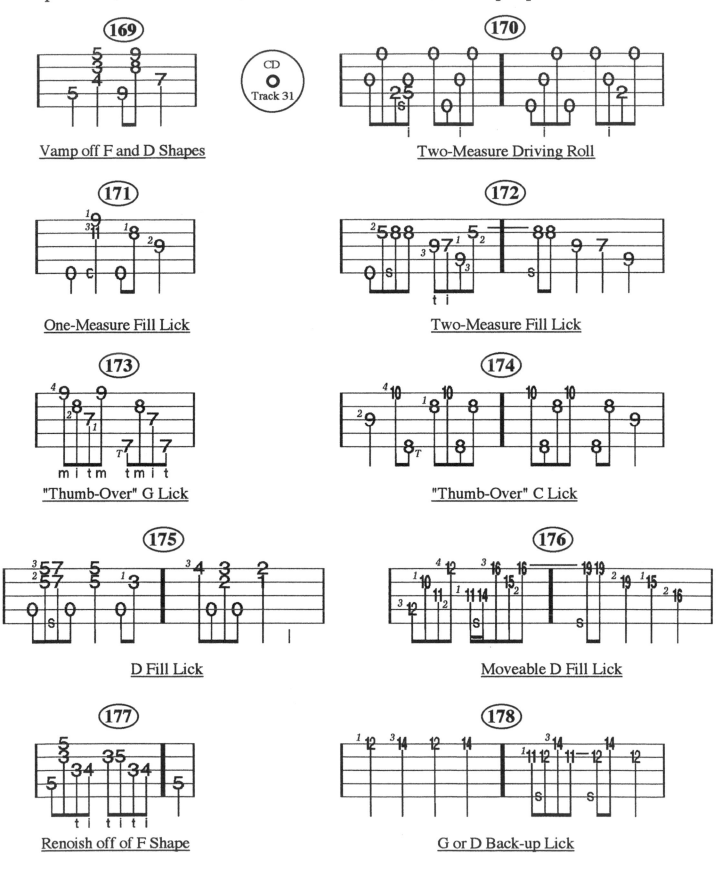

169 Vamp off F and D Shapes

170 Two-Measure Driving Roll

171 One-Measure Fill Lick

172 Two-Measure Fill Lick

173 "Thumb-Over" G Lick

174 "Thumb-Over" C Lick

175 D Fill Lick

176 Moveable D Fill Lick

177 Renoish off of F Shape

178 G or D Back-up Lick

CD
O
Track 31

CHORD PROGRESSION #10

Chord Progression #10 is used for songs like "When The Saints Go Marching In," "The Crawdad Song" and "Mama Don't Allow." The chords for the last line of the progression in this instance will be I V I I. The licks strung together here are more appropriate for back-up than soloing.

Chord Progression #10 (I V I I Ending)

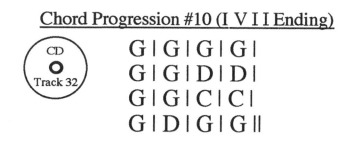

G | G | G | G |
G | G | D | D |
G | G | C | C |
G | D | G | G ||

Chord Progression #10 – Solo (Back-up) 1

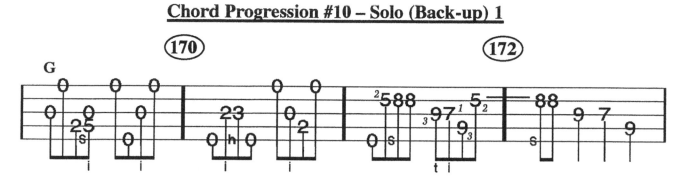

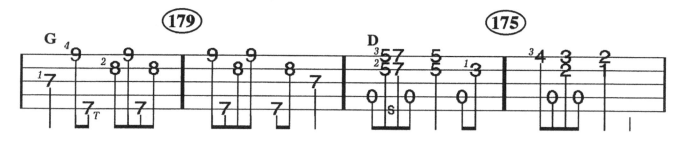

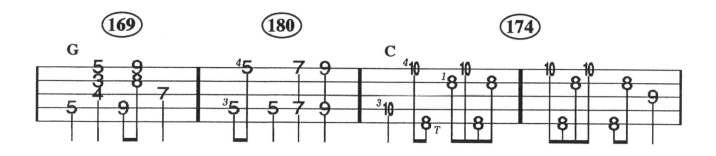

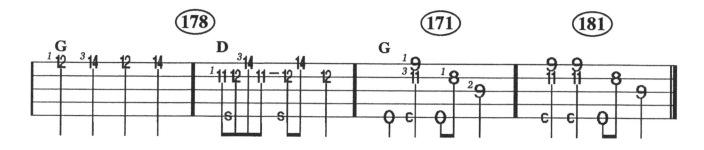

31

PEDAL NOTE LICKS

A *pedal* tone is a note that is repeated throughout a phrase to create rhythmic interplay with the other notes of the phrase. The pedal note can be an open string (# 182) or fretted note (#185).

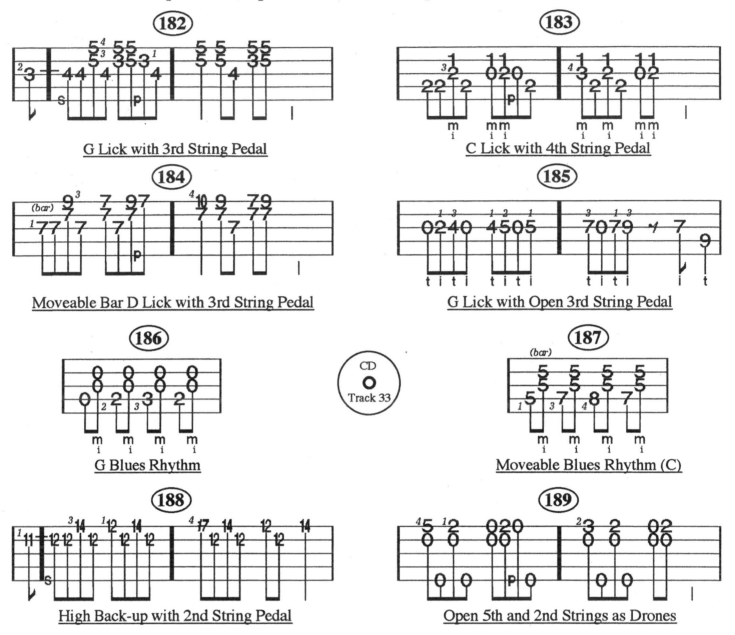

(182) G Lick with 3rd String Pedal

(183) C Lick with 4th String Pedal

(184) Moveable Bar D Lick with 3rd String Pedal

(185) G Lick with Open 3rd String Pedal

(186) G Blues Rhythm

CD
Track 33

(187) Moveable Blues Rhythm (C)

(188) High Back-up with 2nd String Pedal

(189) Open 5th and 2nd Strings as Drones

LICKS WITH 6THS

Notes that are six notes apart in a scale are said to be 6ths. Open-string pedal tones can be inserted between the pairs of fretted 6ths as is demonstrated below.

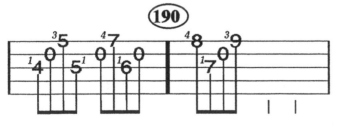

(190) G Lick with 2nd String Pedal

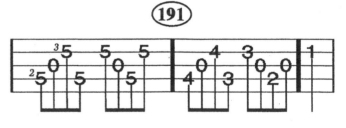

(191) C Lick with 3rd String Pedal

CHORD PROGRESSION #10 – SOLO 2

Here is a second solo for Chord Progression #10, which is also used for "Roll In My Sweet Baby's Arms" and "New River Train." Each has been recorded with a I V I I ending and a V V I I ending for the last four measures. Here we will use the latter ending. Some of the pedal and 6ths licks from page 32 are included in the solo.

Chord Progression #10 (V V I I Ending)

CD O Track 34

G | G | G | G |
G | G | D | D |
G | G | C | C |
G | D | G | G ||

Chord Progression #10 – Solo 2

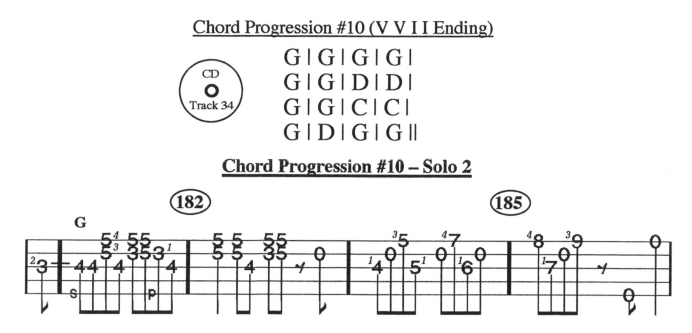

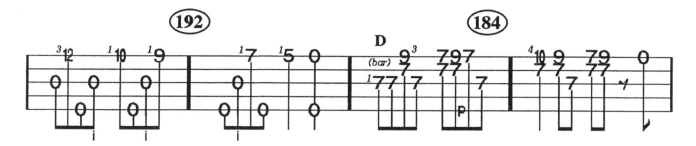

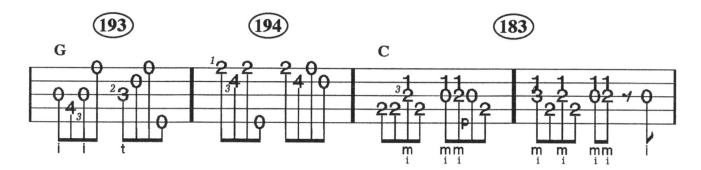

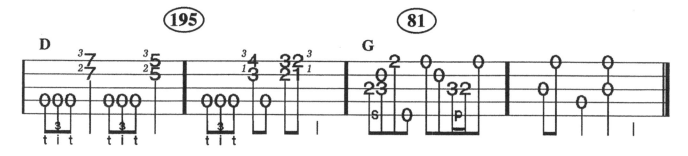

PLAYING LICKS AROUND A MELODY

The primary focus of this book is to help you solo using licks regardless of knowing the melody to a piece. Great players are able to incorporate licks when soloing and still present the melody of the tune. The process for soloing in this manner thus requires you to be familiar with the basic melody of any given song.

The following is offered as an insight as to how licks can ornament the basic melody of a solo. The technique required could be an entire course of study in itself, so view this merely as a sample. Familiarize yourself with the basic melody to "Lonesome Road Blues" below . Then see if you can hear it woven into the solo on page 36. That is then followed by a second solo based more on licks and less on melody (page 37).

Lonesome Road Blues - Basic Melody

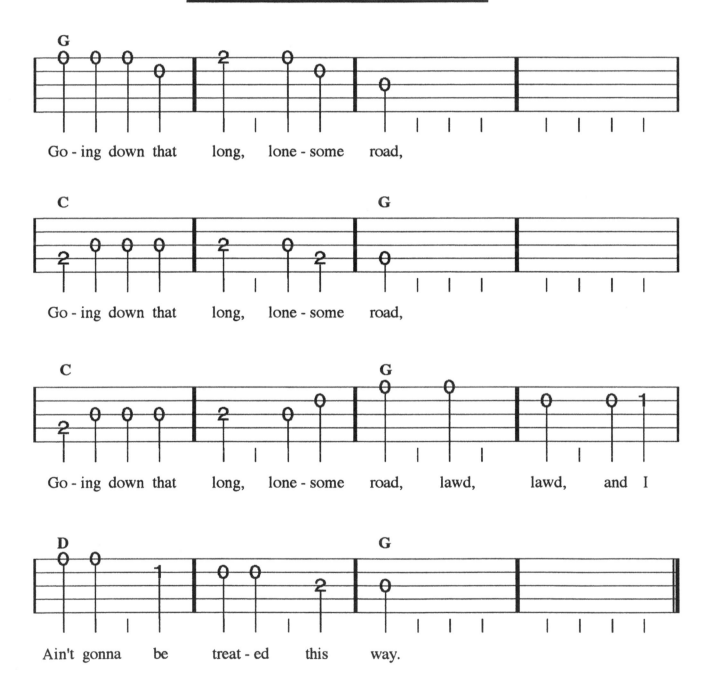

STANDARD BLUEGRASS LICKS

Standard bluegrass licks are those that can be found in numerous solos and are performed by most competent bluegrass players. Below are four common G licks–the first three being permutations of the Foggy Mountain Breakdown lick– then a C lick and D Lick.

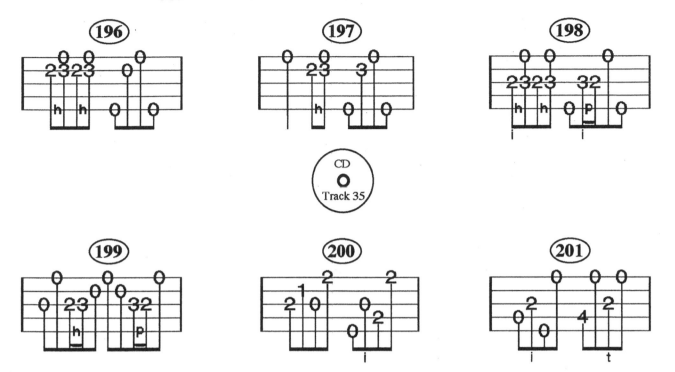

NON-STANDARD BLUEGRASS LICKS

Non-standard licks are those not heard very often and may be associated only with a particular player. Still, they serve their purpose of fitting over particular chords in a given progression.

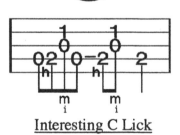

Non-Standard Tag Lick   Non-Standard Transition Lick   Interesting C Lick

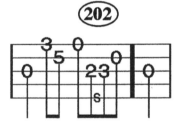

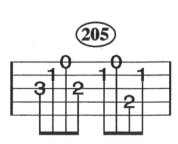

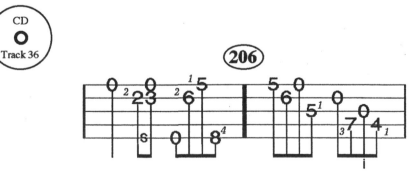

C Modal Lick   Wild Two-Measure D Lick

CHORD PROGRESSION #11

The solo below incorporates the melody of "Lonesome Road Blues." The chord progression is used in other songs, such as "Bluegrass Breakdown." Play the basic melody on page 34 and see if you recognize how the melody is embedded in the licks below. One of the easiest spots to insert licks is in between the vocal phrases.

Chord Progression #11

CD
O
Track 37

```
G | G | G | G |
C | C | G | G |
C | C | G | G |
D | D | G | G ||
```

Chord Progression #11 – Solo 1

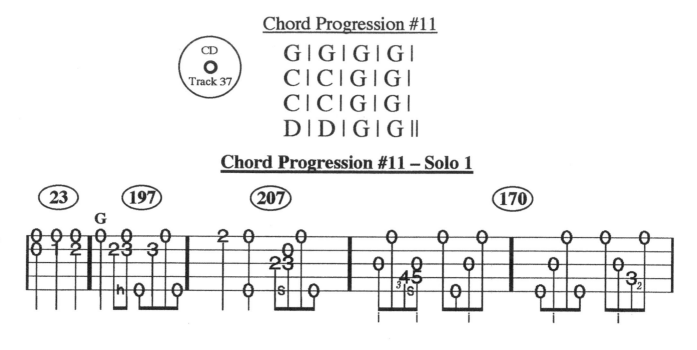

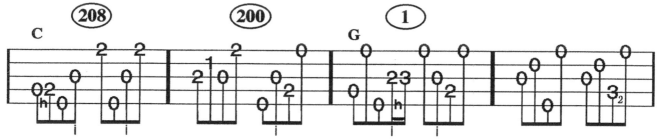

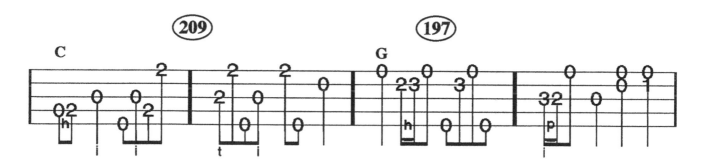

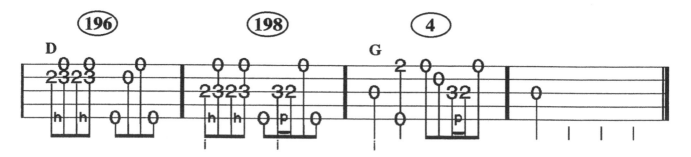

Let's take another pass at Progression #11. Here there is more inclination to insert licks, standard or non-standard, that fit the background chords than adhering to the melody of "Lonesome Road Blues." Such solos are usually best played as a "second break" where the melody has been previously established.

Chord Progression #11

G | G | G | G |
C | C | G | G |
C | C | G | G |
D | D | G | G ‖

Chord Progression #11 – Solo 2

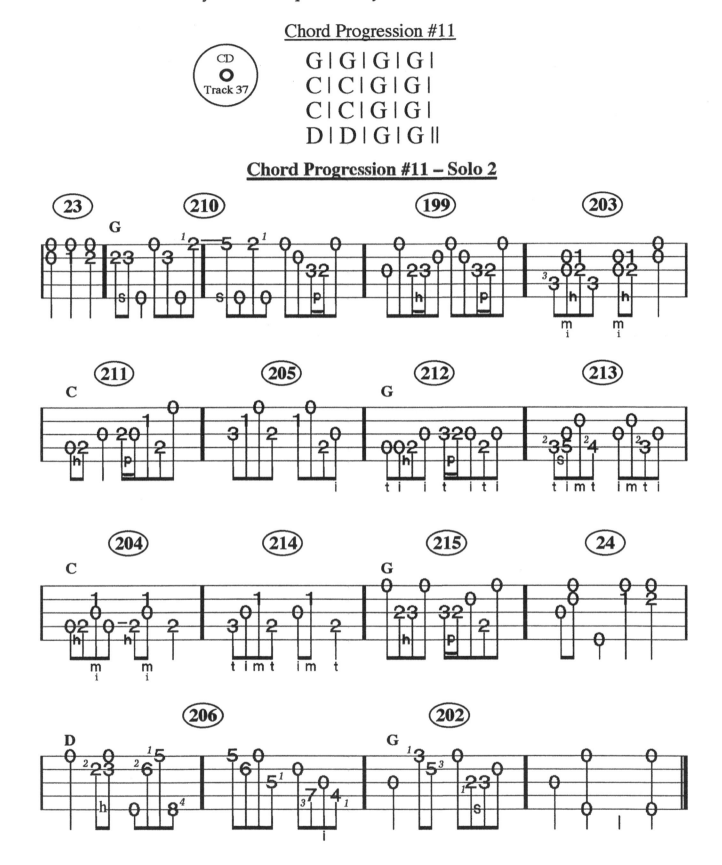

MOVEABLE LICKS

Any lick comprised solely of fretted notes can be relocated to work against different chords. The C licks below moved up two frets would become D Licks. #220 below is lick #176 (page 30) moved back seven frets. The 5th string is occasionally sounded in a moveable phrase (#219),

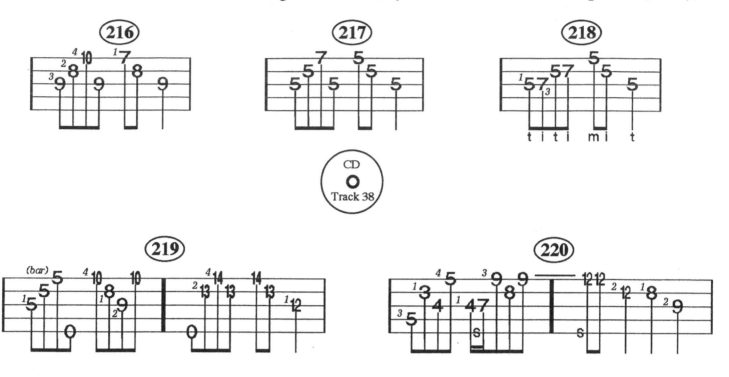

FINISHING LICKS

A *finishing* lick creates the anticipation of a conclusion. One expects to hear the open 3rd string after lick #221. Finishing licks are often followed by tag licks in vocal tunes.

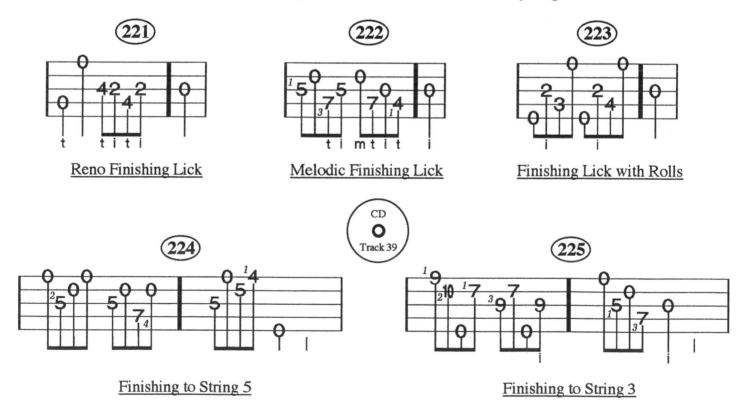

Reno Finishing Lick

Melodic Finishing Lick

Finishing Lick with Rolls

Finishing to String 5

Finishing to String 3

CHORD PROGRESSION #12

This new progression gives you a chance to practice some of the moveable licks and finishing licks found on page 38. Progression #12 forms the basis for songs such as "Boil 'Em Cabbage Down," "Dixie Hoedown" and "Dooley."

Chord Progression #12

CD
Track 40

G | C | G | D |
G | C | G D | G ||

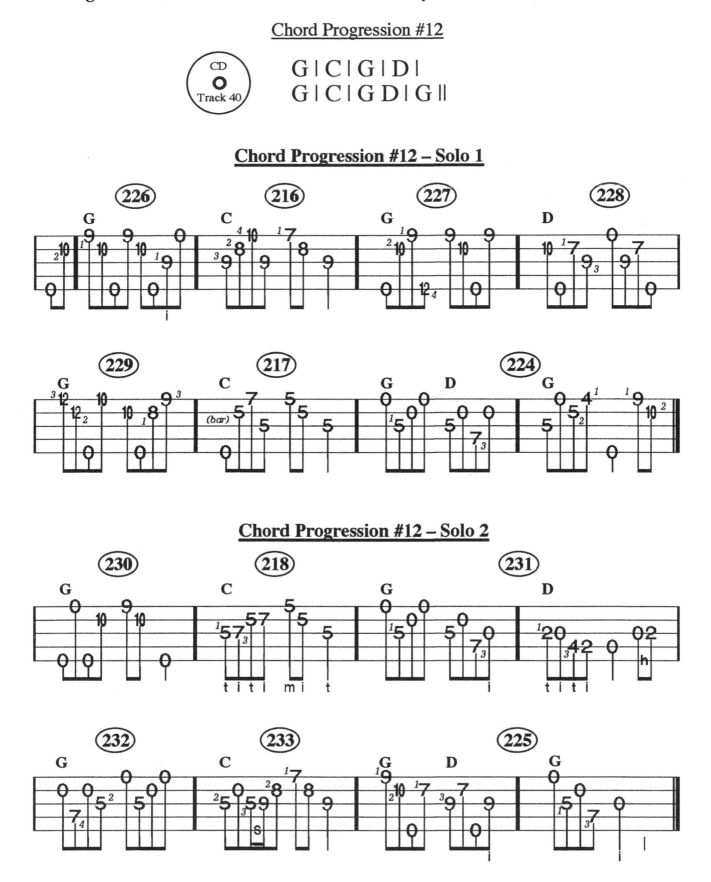

39

SOLOING IN THE KEY OF C

You already have enough licks to solo in the key of C as we have licks for the I (C) and V (G) chord. The adaptation you will need to make is to resolve your solos to the note C. You will need a few C tag licks, some of which just imitate licks from G.

C Tag Licks

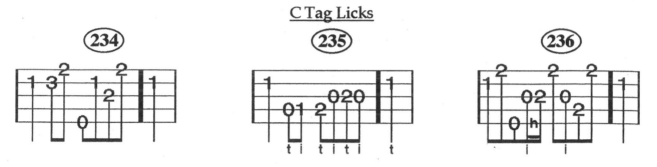

KEY OF C MELODIC SCALE

We have experienced small pieces of the key of C scale before when the note F, either on the 3rd fret of string 4 or 1, was added as a blue note. There are more shifts required in the left hand to manage the C melodic scale than the G.

Two-Octave C Melodic Scale (C Roots are Circled)

You will need to dampen unwanted open strings when resolving to the 5th fret on string 3 (#237). C licks can be developed in any of our previous categories. Some licks will mimic common G licks (#238). Others will combine parts of C chords from various positions on the neck (#240).

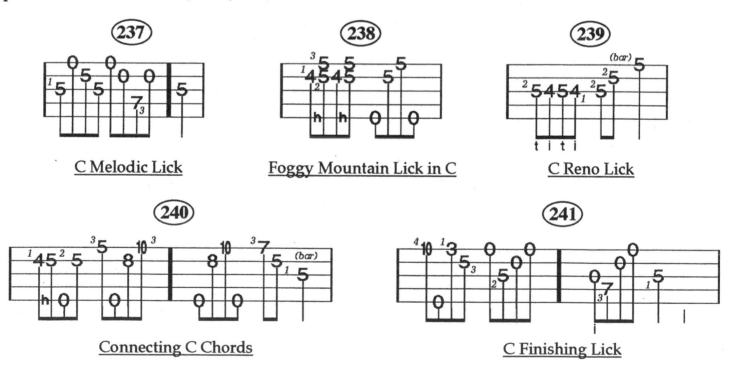

C Melodic Lick   Foggy Mountain Lick in C   C Reno Lick

Connecting C Chords   C Finishing Lick

CHORD PROGRESSION #1 - KEY OF C

Let's return to our very first chord progression that only has I and V chords, but this time play it in the key of C. "Carter's Blues" and "Jambalya" use this progression. These solos contain several previously learned licks. Remember, when soloing in the key of C, the sound should work its way back to the C root either on the 1st fret of string 2, or the 5th fret of string 3.

Chord Progression #1

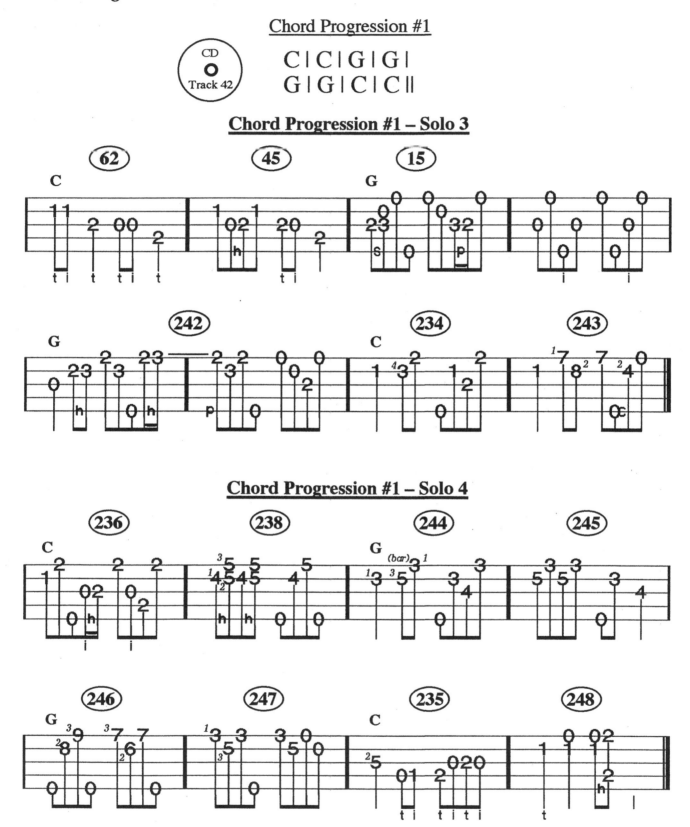

F LICKS

F is the IV chord in the key of C. Blue notes Ab and Eb (flatted 3rd and flatted 7th) are often included in F licks in addition to notes taken directly from the F pentatonic scale (F, G, A, C, D).

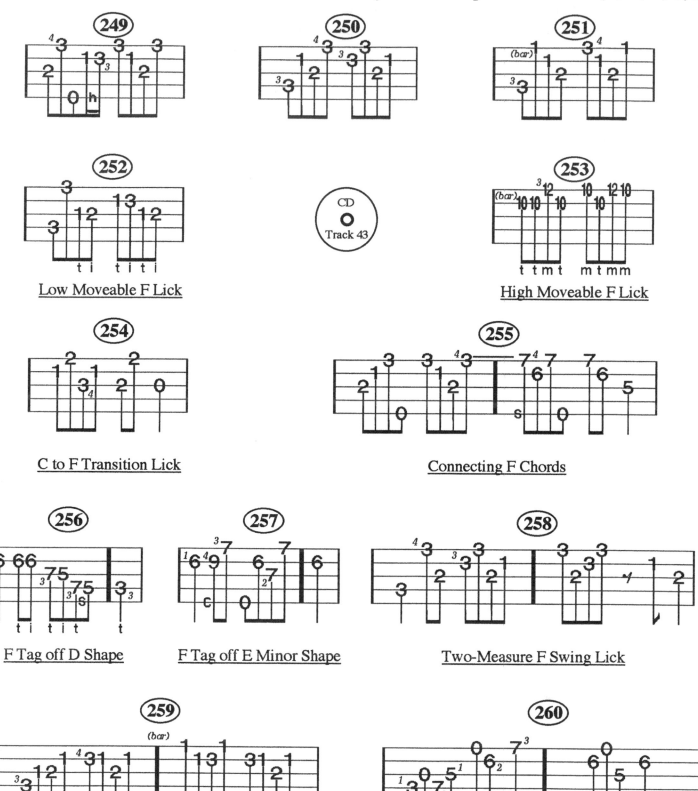

Low Moveable F Lick

High Moveable F Lick

C to F Transition Lick

Connecting F Chords

F Tag off D Shape

F Tag off E Minor Shape

Two-Measure F Swing Lick

F Boogie Lick

F Pentatonic Melodic Lick

42

CHORD PROGRESSION #4 – KEY OF C

We can now put our C, F and G licks together in Progression #4. Tunes like "Beautiful Brown Eyes" and "Blue Moon Of Kentucky" fit this progression. This will give you a couple of opportunities to insert your F licks. Just a reminder that we are still using standard open G tuning even though the song is in the key of C.

Chord Progression #4

CD
O
Track 44

C | C | F | F |
C | C | G | G |
C | C | F | F |
C | G | C | C ||

Chord Progression #4 – Solo 3

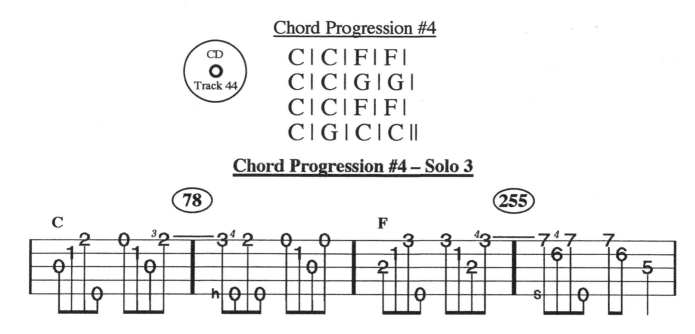

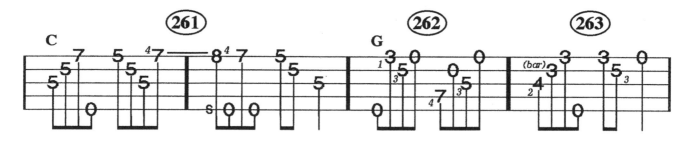

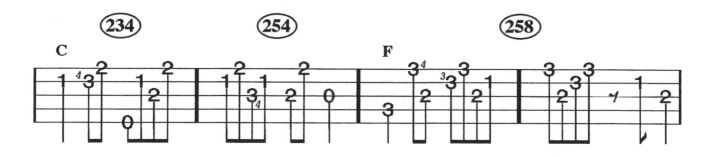

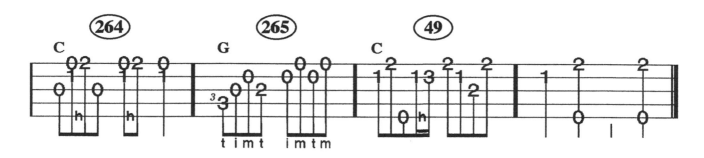

CHROMATIC LICKS

Chromatic simply refers to those notes that fill the space between the normal scale tones. Our previously discussed flatted 3rds and 7ths fall in this category. Pretty much anything goes as long as the added notes reach a logical conclusion (see #267).

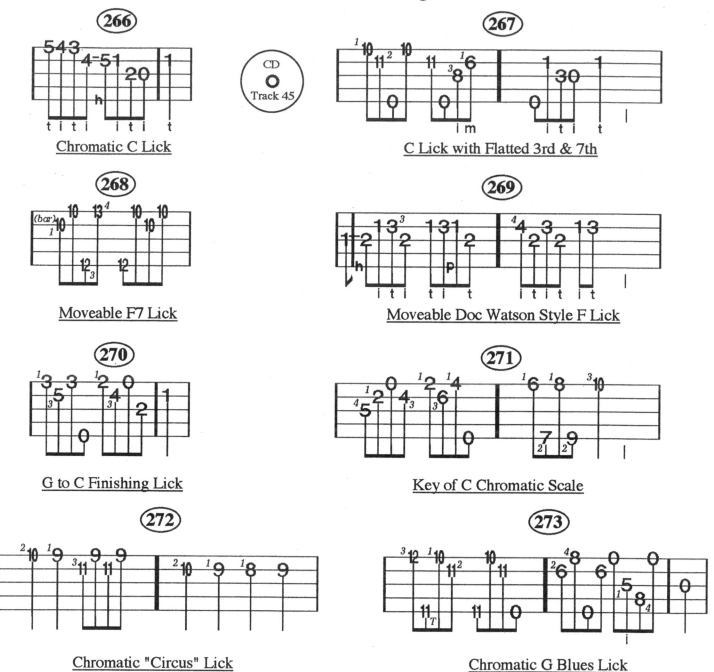

Chromatic C Lick

C Lick with Flatted 3rd & 7th

Moveable F7 Lick

Moveable Doc Watson Style F Lick

G to C Finishing Lick

Key of C Chromatic Scale

Chromatic "Circus" Lick

Chromatic G Blues Lick

12 BAR BLUES – KEY OF C

Many blues phrases with pick-ups and anticipatory notes along with chromatic licks occur in the 12 Bar Blues on page 45. The progression is used in "Honky Tonk Swing."

Chord Progression #7

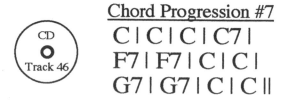

C | C | C | C7 |
F7 | F7 | C | C |
G7 | G7 | C | C ||

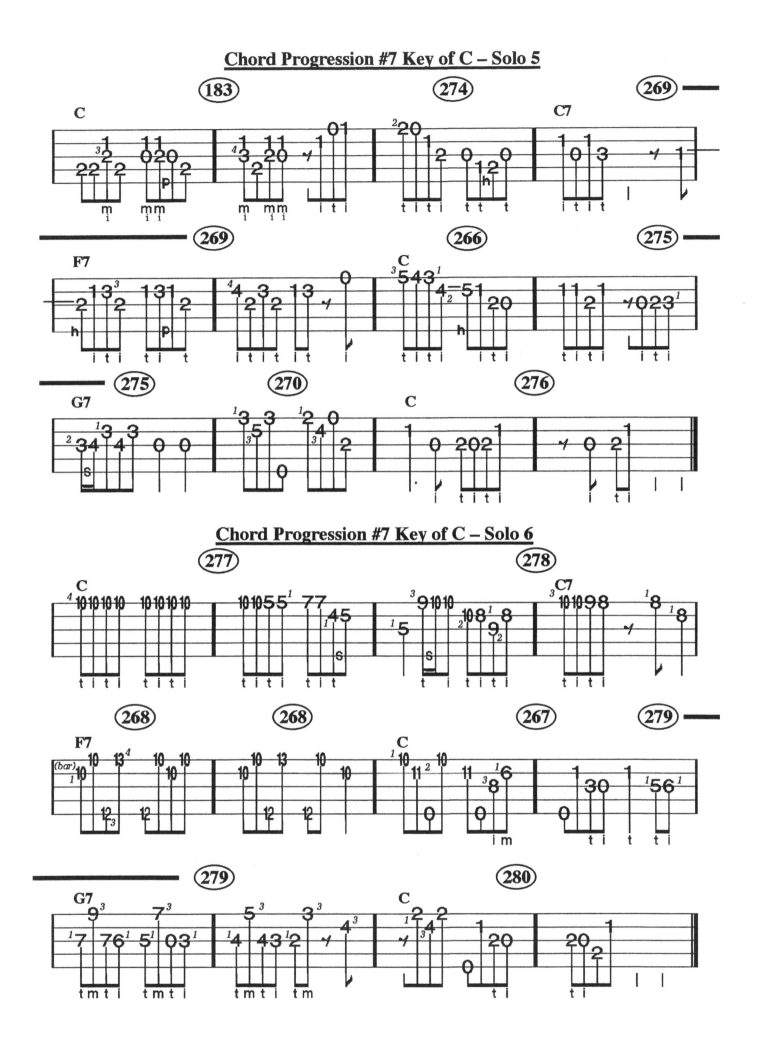

EMBELLISHING A FIDDLE TUNE

After hearing the straight melody several times in a jam, it is nice to vary it. To do this, focus on keeping important melody notes and any unique syncopated phrasing associated with the piece. Let's try it with "Beaumont Rag" – Chord Progression #13. Note that guitarists like this in C, whereas fiddlers play it in F. It begins on the V chord.

Chord Progression #13

CD
O
Track 47

G7 | G7 | C | C |
G7 | G7 | C | C |
G7 | G7 | C | C7 |
F | C | G7 | C ||

Chord Progression #13 – Solo 1

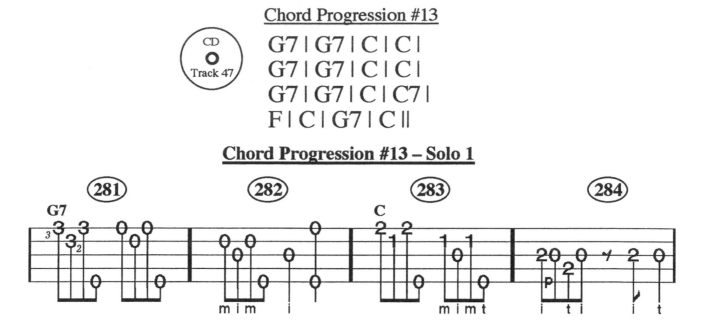

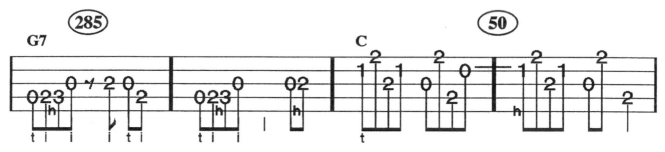

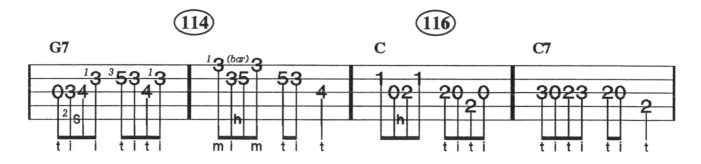

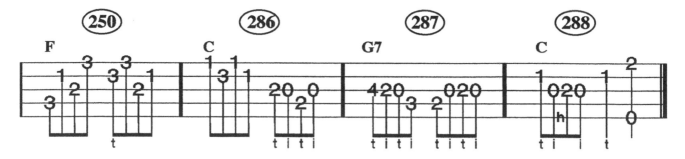

QUOTES

Certain songs, especially rags, lend themselves to finding a spot to throw in a couple of measures from another melody. Such brief melodic statements are called *quotes*. The beginning of "Sailor's Hornpipe" is often used for this purpose. The "Circus" theme is used in this second pass of "Beaumont Rag," which includes a couple sequential licks.

Chord Progression #13

G7 | G7 | C | C |
G7 | G7 | C | C |
G7 | G7 | C | C7 |
F | C | G7 | C ||

Chord Progression #13 – Solo 2

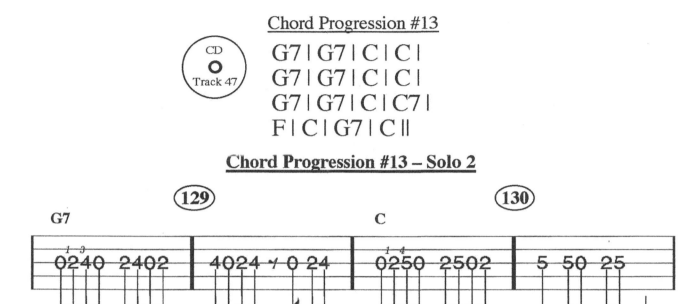

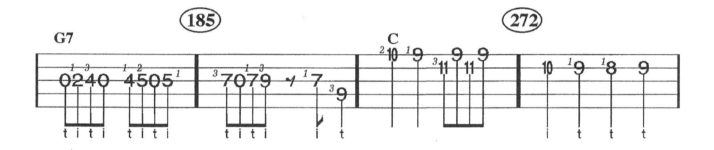

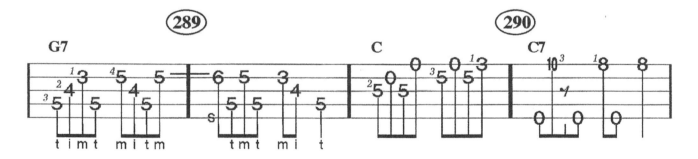

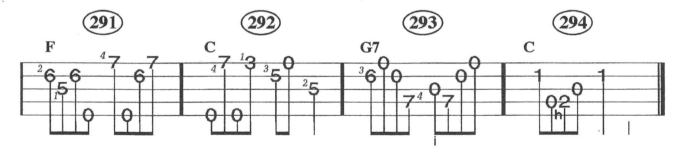

SOLOING IN THE KEY OF D

We've seen plenty of D licks as the V chord of the key of G. Any F notes–fret 3 on string 1 or 4–are blue notes. D major or D pentatonic scales could be played at the second position with finger 1 playing fret 2. Let's look at a couple of D tag licks to get started.

D Tag Licks

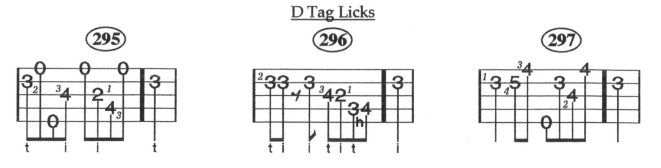

KEY OF D MELODIC SCALE

The only note different in the D major scale versus the G scale is the note C#, although it produces an entirely new "feel" with its fingerings.

Two-Octave D Melodic Scale (D Roots are Circled)

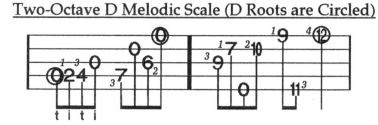

RETUNING THE 5TH STRING

You may have noticed the open 5th string sounded a little "off" in lick #297. Tuning the 5th string to A will sound better for Scruggs style licks, whereas you'd need to keep it at G for melodic licks.

Scruggs Licks–5th String A

Melodic Licks–5th String G

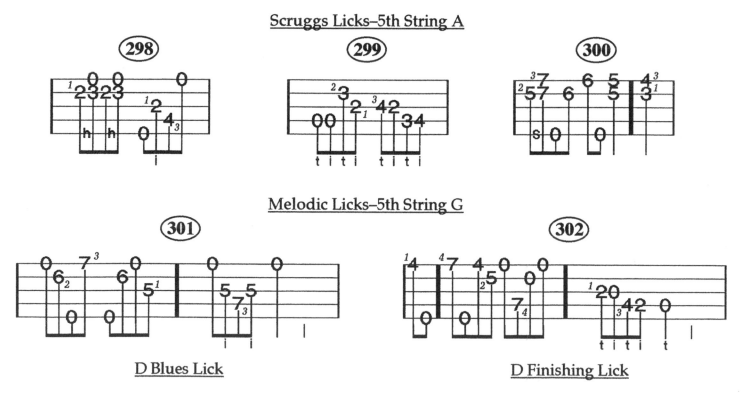

D Blues Lick   D Finishing Lick

CHORD PROGRESSION #14 – KEY OF D

Several fiddle tunes, like "Eighth Of January" and "Black Mountain Rag," have a four-measure section of a continuous I chord with a quick V I ending like Progression #14. This gives you lots of chances to insert D licks–with the 5th string tuned to either A or G.

Chord Progression #14

D | D | D | A D :‖

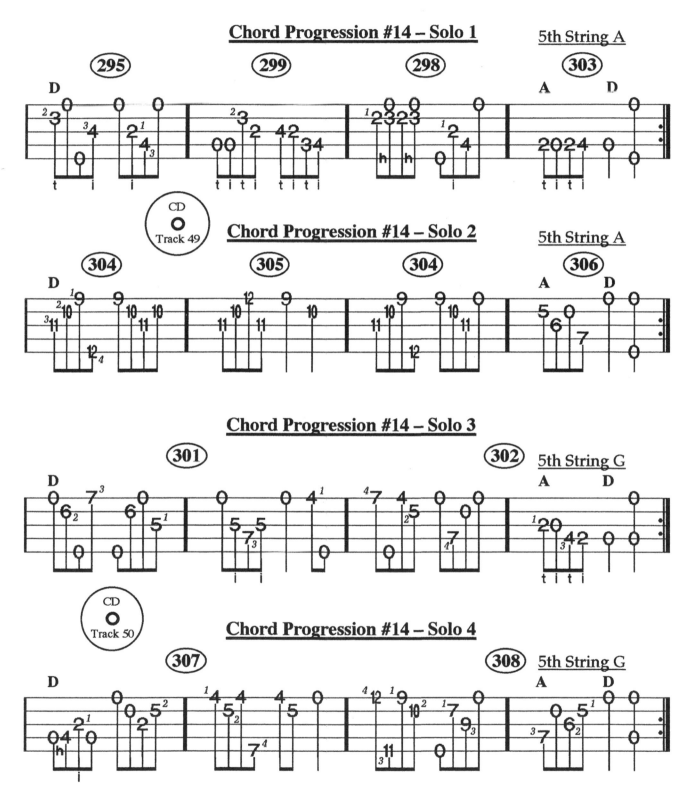

A LICKS

A is the V chord in the key of D. Blue notes C and G (flatted 3rd and flatted 7th) are often found in A licks. All of these licks are performed with the 5th string tuned to G (standard tuning).

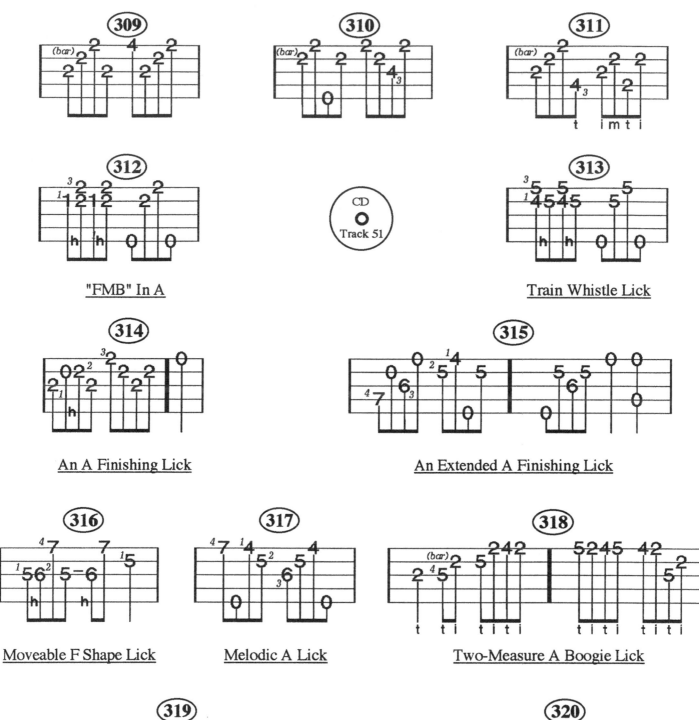

"FMB" In A

Train Whistle Lick

An A Finishing Lick

An Extended A Finishing Lick

Moveable F Shape Lick

Melodic A Lick

Two-Measure A Boogie Lick

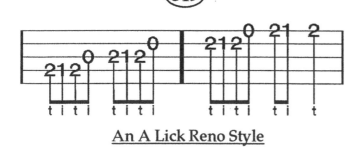

An A Lick Reno Style

An A Lick off Moveable Chord Shapes

Progression #5 is used for tunes such as "This Land Is Your Land" and Part B of "Turkey Knob." Just a reminder that the progression begins on the IV chord. This will give you a couple of opportunities to insert your D, G and A licks.

Chord Progression #5

CD
Track 52

G | G | D | D |
A | A | D | D ||

Chord Progression #5 – Solo 3

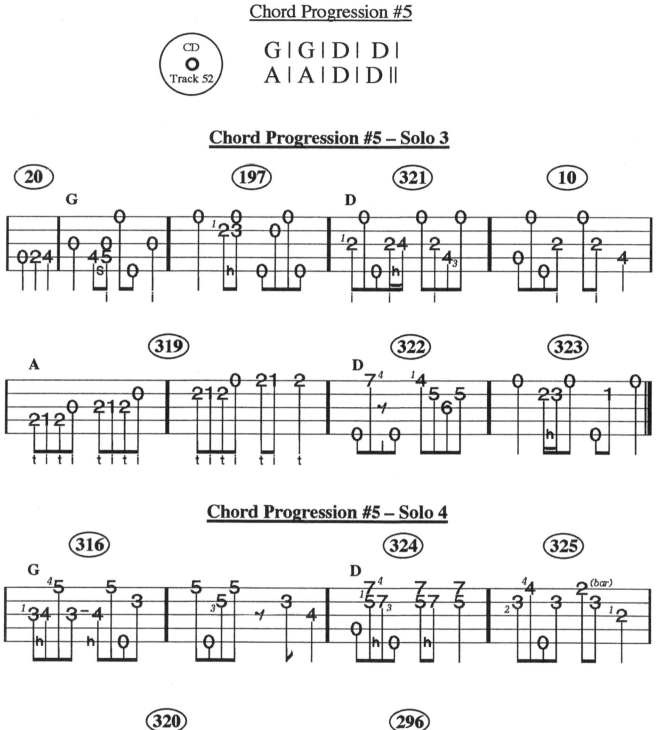

Chord Progression #5 – Solo 4

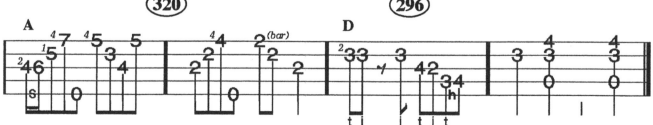

D PENTATONIC BLUES SCALE

Like the key of G (page 20), the five note D pentatonic blues scale contains scale tones 1, b3, 4, 5 and b7. The minor sound is often used to play over major or 7th chords. Notice how the first licks play off of positions for F chords although they are *D* blues licks.

D Pentatonic Blues Scale (roots are circled)

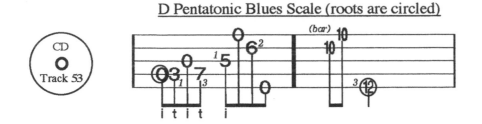

One-Measure D Pentatonic Blues Licks

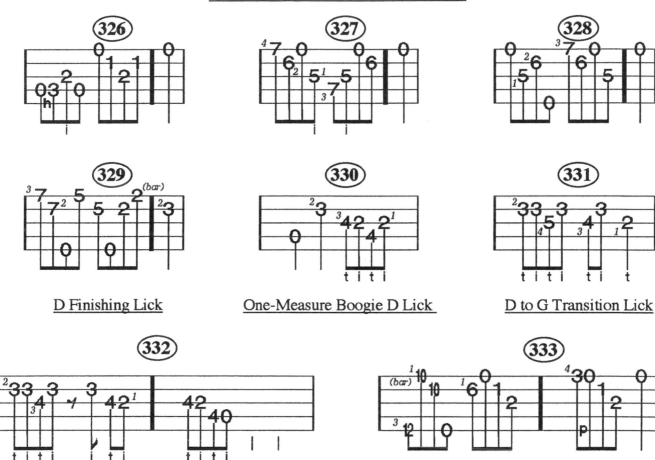

D Finishing Lick

One-Measure Boogie D Lick

D to G Transition Lick

Extended Swing Tag Lick

Extended D Blues Lick

12 BAR BLUES – KEY OF D

Progression #7 provides a chance to practice using your D blues, boogie and swing phrases. The progression is used for the tune "Bluegrass Stomp."

Chord Progression #7

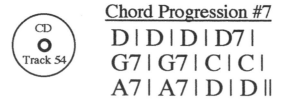

D | D | D | D7 |
G7 | G7 | C | C |
A7 | A7 | D | D ||

Chord Progression #7 Key of D – Solo 7

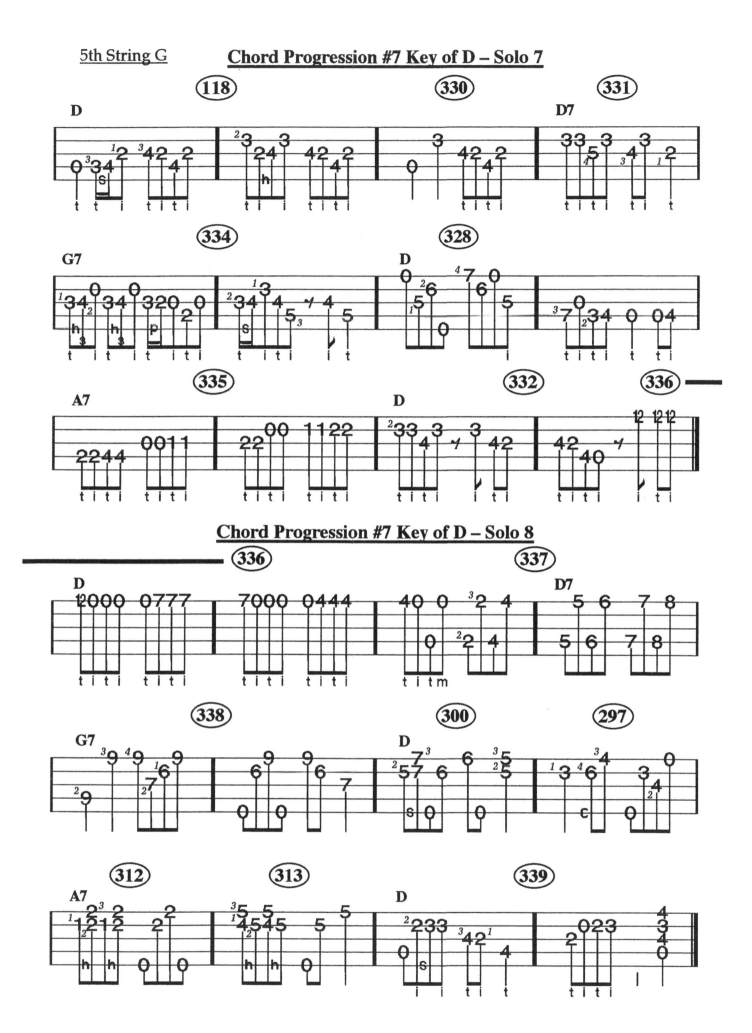

Chord Progression #7 Key of D – Solo 8

THE II CHORD

It is beyond the scope of this book to cover all the chord possibilities one might encounter in a bluegrass progression. Chords beyond I, IV and V are sometimes simply referred to as *off* chords. One of the most common off chords is a major chord built on the 2nd scale degree of the key. It is safe to assume that any II chord in a bluegrass progression will be followed by a V.

II – V – I TURNAROUND–KEY OF D

Songs that include a II may kick off with a II – V – I turnaround. This would be the equivalent of the line "I wonder how the old folks are at home" from the song "Homestead On The Farm." Since the II chord in the key of D is E, we'll need an E lick and A and D licks to create a turnaround. The accompaniment should come in on the downbeat of the II chord.

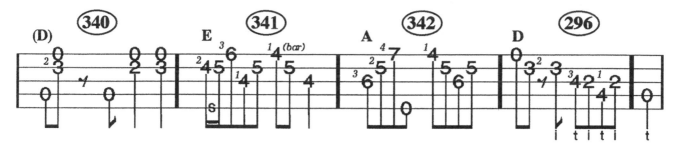

E LICKS

In addition to the II in D being E, E is the V of A. So let's look at some E licks–most will avoid the 5th string and many will be moveable licks.

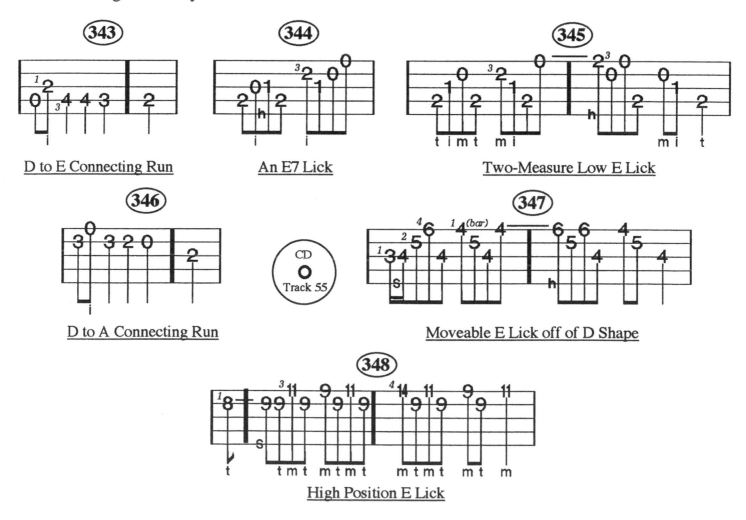

D to E Connecting Run

An E7 Lick

Two-Measure Low E Lick

D to A Connecting Run

CD Track 55

Moveable E Lick off of D Shape

High Position E Lick

CHORD PROGRESSIONS #s 15 & 16

The II chord is often used during a chorus or bridge with the final chord usually a V. This is then followed by a recap from a previous part of the song. Progression #15 is used in "Old Home Place" and "I'm Using My Bible For A Road Map." Progression #16 could be played to begin the second part of "Lonesome Fiddle Blues."

Chord Progression #15 – Key of D

V | V | I | I |
II | II | V | V ||

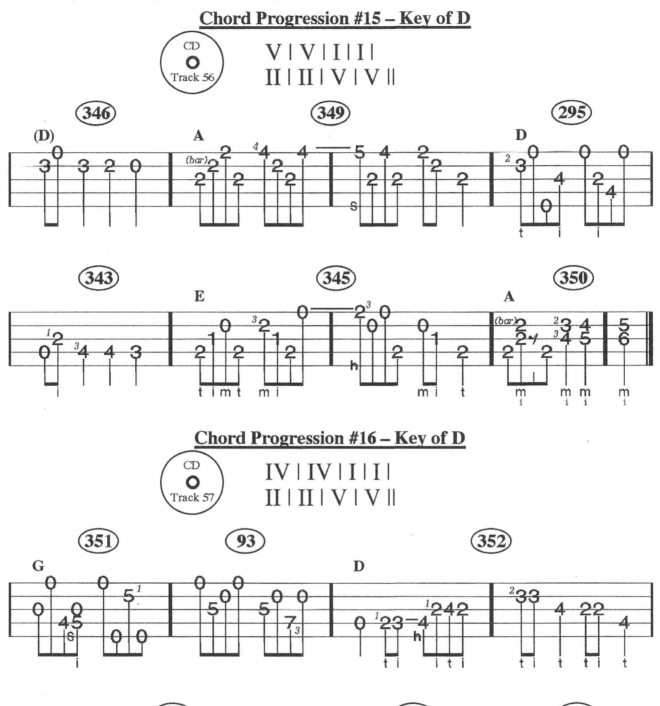

Chord Progression #16 – Key of D

IV | IV | I | I |
II | II | V | V ||

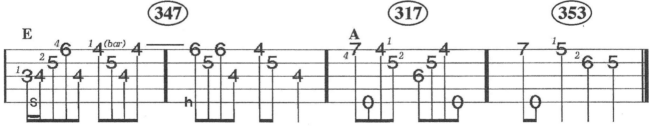

STANDARD HIGH POSITION LICKS

We now return to the key of G. We've seen many standard down the neck licks, most notably on page 35. There were some fairly standard high position licks presented in the back-up licks section on page 30. There are many more that you will want to have at your disposal.

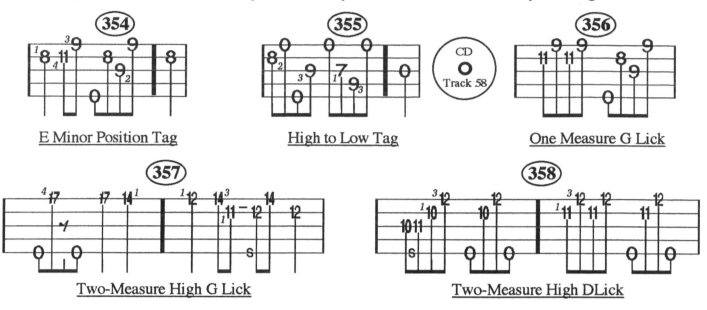

CHORD PROGRESSION #17

This new progression will give you a chance to focus on your high licks. It could represent the chords for "Salty Dog." Many other songs, such as "Don't Let Your Deal Go Down," follow the pattern, but replace the first measure G with an E chord. This is a VI II V I progression.

Chord Progression #17

G | E | A | A |
D | D | G | G ||

Chord Progression #17 – Solo 1

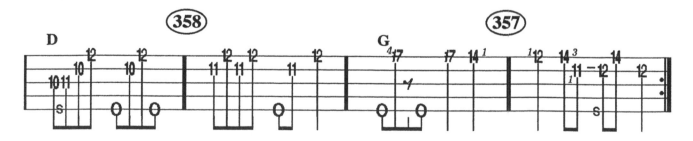

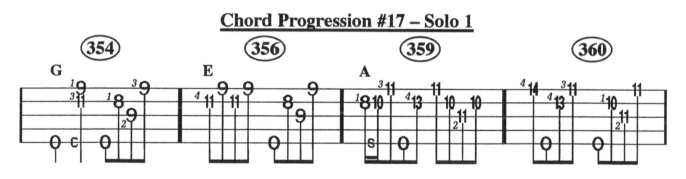

THE FLATTED 7TH CHORD

Progression #18 makes use of a *flatted* 7th chord, meaning the 7th note that actually belongs in the G scale is F#, but the chord is built off F natural. Several standard licks, as well as some new non-standard licks, have been inserted for practice. Chord Progression #18 can be used for the song "Little Maggie."

Challenge: Find the chords for the progression in the key of D and create a solo for it.

Chord Progression #18

CD
O
Track 60

G | G | F | F |
G | D | G | G ||

Chord Progression #18 – Solo 1

This "choke" lick sounds good against G, C and D chords

Chord Progression #18 – Solo 2

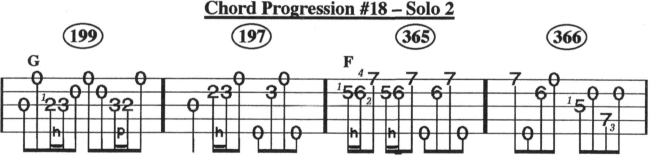

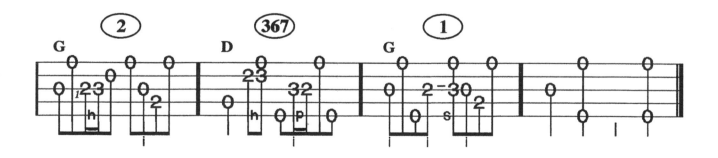

PRACTICE LOOPS

Success in incorporating new licks is determined by how you practice. Playing solos from beginning to end doesn't produce the best results, as some parts will remain rough. It is best to first play a lick you are learning over and over in a *loop*.

A memorized phrase should then be practiced in context. Again, rather than practicing entire solos, form a loop with the lick plus a couple of other measures. First play the somewhat standard last line of "Salt Creek" (#s 368 & 369). Then, after loop practicing #s 370 & 371, try each one in context by using it instead of 369.

Last Line of "Salt Creek" – Key of A: Capo 2

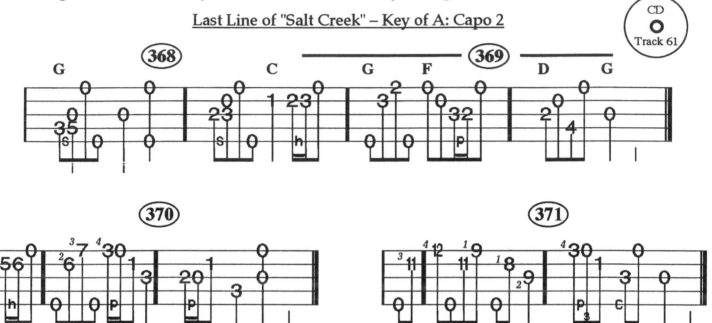

Now try the concept again, but with some licks that can substitute for the finishing lick of "Soldier's Joy."

Last Line of "Soldier's Joy" – Key of D, No Capo

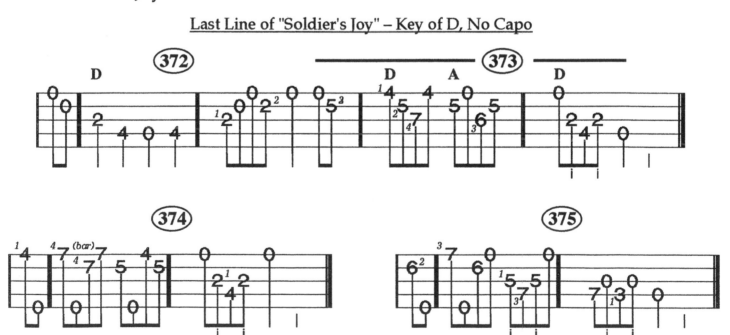

FINAL ENDINGS

Instrumental songs, especially fiddle tunes, often conclude with a fancy ending. Such endings are usually four measures and most consist of two licks–a *pre-ending* and *final ending*. Most begin with pick-up notes on beat 4 and conclude with a V I ending. Try to develop your own final endings once you understand the concept.

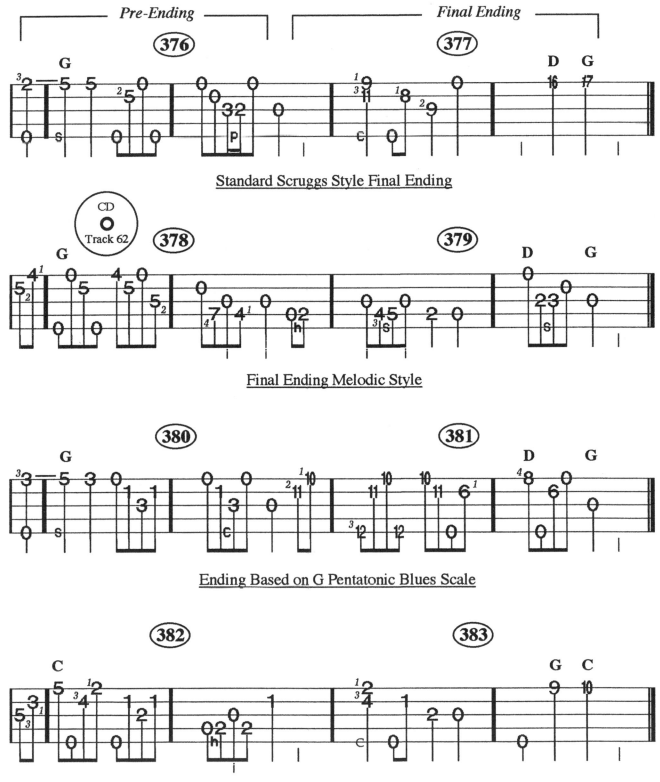

Standard Scruggs Style Final Ending

Final Ending Melodic Style

Ending Based on G Pentatonic Blues Scale

Key of C Final Ending

BONUS SONG SECTION – NINE POUND HAMMER

Now for real-world examples of how to use licks when soloing. Chord Progression #19 forms the basis for the song "Nine Pound Hammer," a popular tune played at bluegrass jam sessions. The banjo is often called on to kick off the song before the singer comes in. The licks you choose to use for such opening solos should contain a healthy dose of melody notes and standard licks, as discussed on pages 34 and 35.

Challenge: Once familiar with the solos below, try swapping out some of the licks.

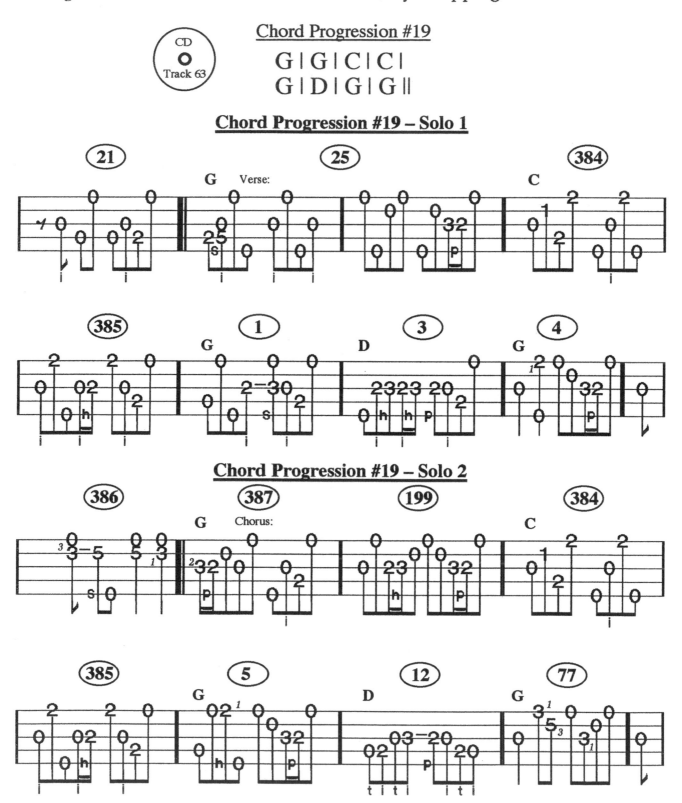

NINE POUND HAMMER (Continued)

Often in a jam session you will get a "second break" on a song, especially if you were the one to kick it off. While often such solos still hint at the melody, this is an opportunity to "show what you got," so to speak. The guiding principal here is to make sure the licks you choose to play fit over the chords of the progression. Notice the inclusion of a sequence of licks (page 26).

Challenge: Again, once familiar with these solos, try swapping out some of the licks.

Chord Progression #19

G | G | C | C |
G | D | G | G ‖

Chord Progression #19 – Solo 3

Chord Progression #19 – Solo 4

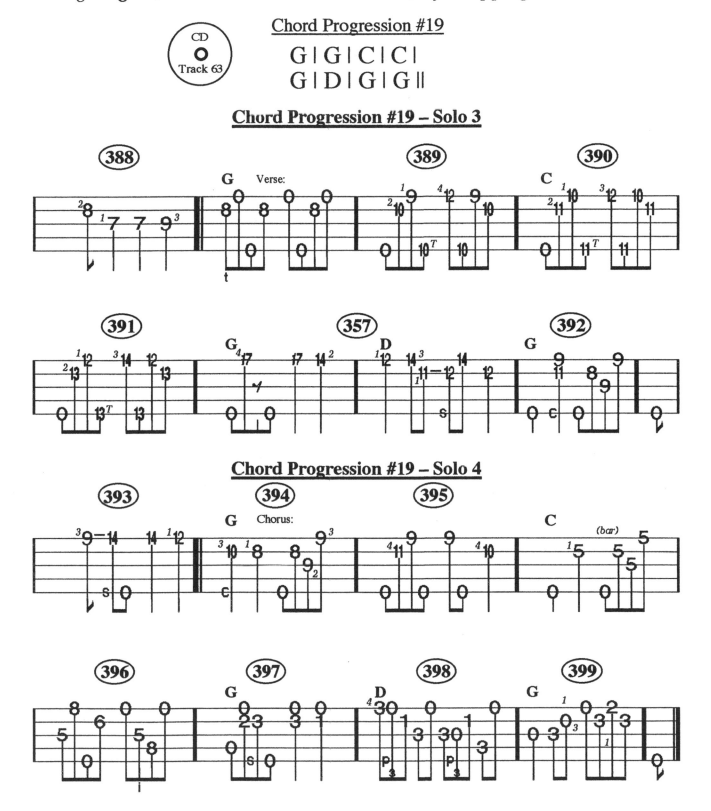

61

CHORD PROGRESSION #20 – HAYSTACK RAG

Progression #20 is 32 measures long. I often call it "The Polka Progression," as many polkas follow this pattern, such as "Beer Barrel Polka" and "Just Because." A song on my *Rapid Transit* CD, "Haystack Rag," is also based on this pattern. Rather than recreate that melody, I have strung together licks from the book to form a nice *second* solo.

(First Half) Chord Progression #20 - Key of C

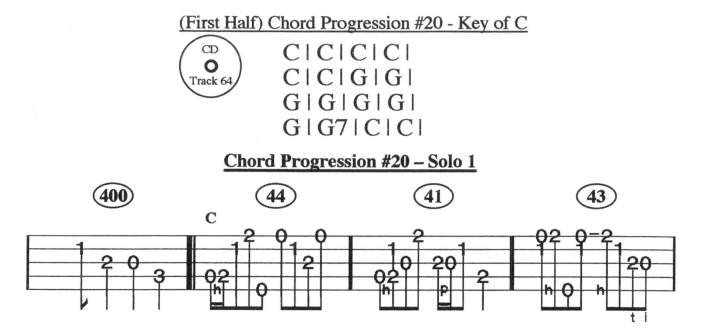

C | C | C | C |
C | C | G | G |
G | G | G | G |
G | G7 | C | C |

Chord Progression #20 – Solo 1

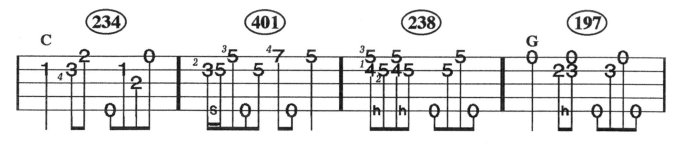

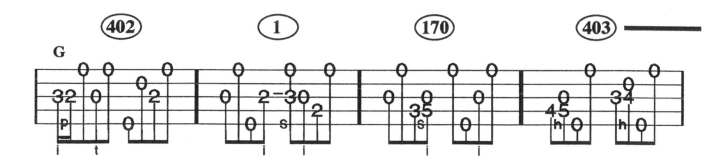

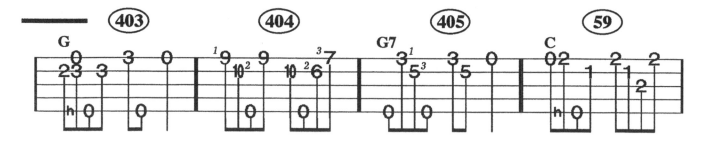

62

HAYSTACK RAG (Continued)

We'll stretch out a little more as we continue in the second half of Progression #20. Both pages combined create a non-stop 32 measure solo. The F# chord in the next to last line is a diminished chord. Much of this part of the solo is playing off of chord positions with most of the licks being new. A melodic flourish brings it all to a nice conclusion.

(Second Half) Chord Progression #20 - Key of C

CD
O
Track 64

C | C | C | C |
C | C7 | F | F |
F | F#° | C | A |
D | G | C | C ||

Chord Progression #20 – Solo 1 Continued

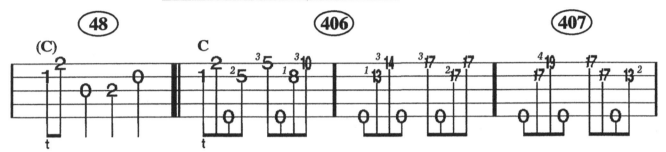

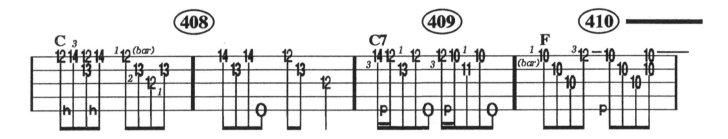

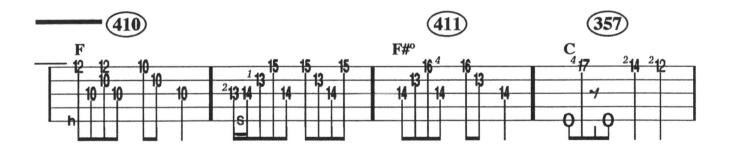

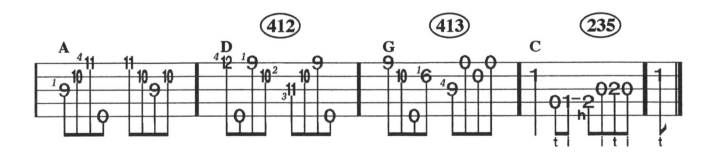

BLACK MOUNTAIN RAG – Parts A & B

The two common keys for this famous fiddle tune are D and A. The following is in the key of A (Capo 2) and is taken from the first break I play on the tune on my *Rise & Shine* album. A lot of standard, yet somewhat flashy, licks are woven into the melody.

Chord Progression #14 – Key of A: Capo 2

G | G | G | G | D G :‖

Chord Progression #14 – Solo 5

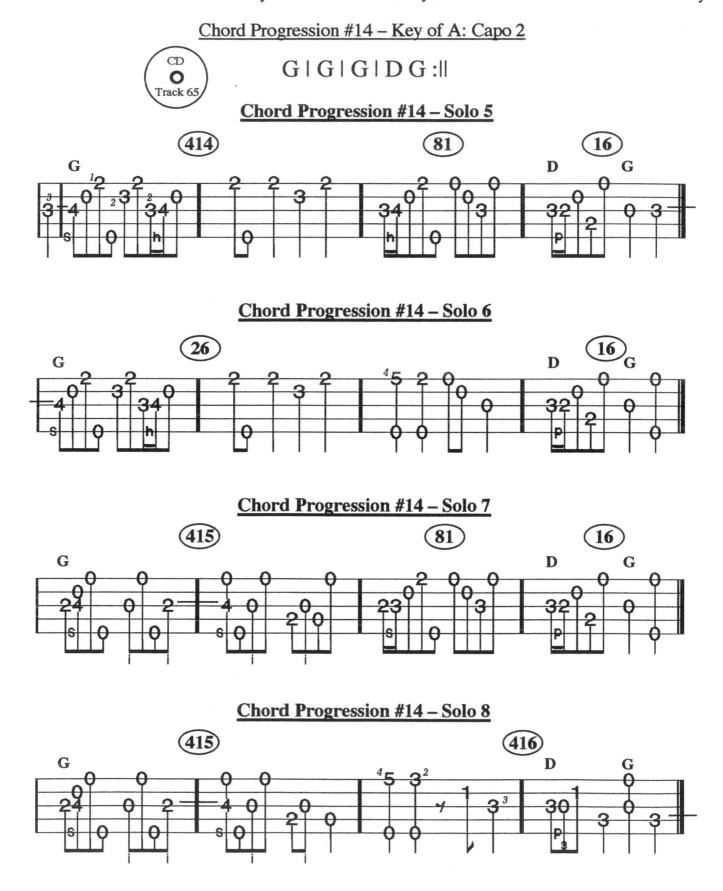

Chord Progression #14 – Solo 6

Chord Progression #14 – Solo 7

Chord Progression #14 – Solo 8

BLACK MOUNTAIN RAG – Part C

This third part works its way through I, IV and V chords, rather than just the I and V of the previous parts. Remember, this is a first break, we're still eluding regularly to the melody. You may wish to conclude the piece with a final ending (see page 59).

Note: Some licks may have changed a note or two from the originals in all three parts.

Chord Progression #4 – Key of A: Capo 2

CD O Track 65

```
G | G | C | C |
G | G | D | D |
G | G | C | C |
G | D | G | G ||
```

Chord Progression #4 – Solo 4

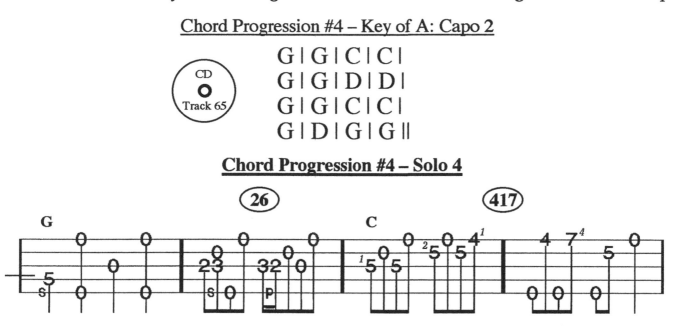

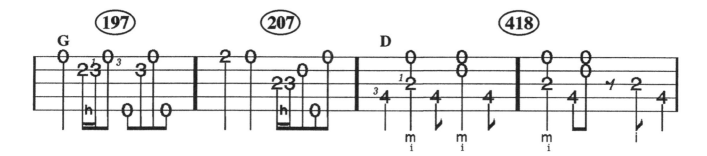

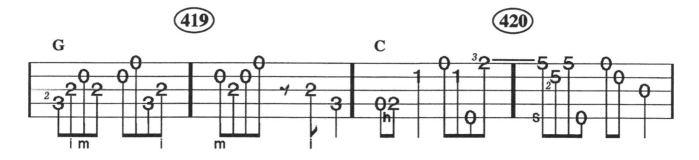

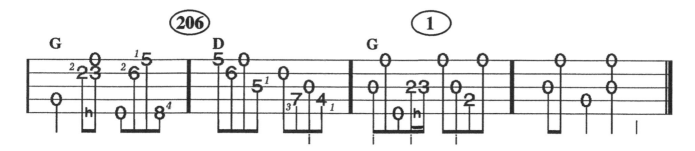

Symbol	Name	Explanation	
|	Measure Line	Separates notes into an equal number of beats	
||	Double Bar	Marks start or end of a section	**The Left-Hand Fingers** (palm up)
||:	Begin Repeat	Marks start of part played twice	1 2 3 4
:||	End Repeat	Marks end of repeated section	
1.	1st Ending	Play this ending 1st time through	
2.	2nd Ending	Play this ending 2nd time through	
$\frac{3}{4}$	Time Signature	Top # = # of beats per measure; Bottom # = the type of note that gets 1 count	
			The Right-Hand Fingers (palm up) M I T
♪	Eighth Note	Receives 1/2 count	
|	Quarter Note	Receives 1 count	
⊔	8ths Beam	Count 2 per beat	
⊟	16ths Beam	Count 4 per beat	
3	Triplet	Count 3 per beat	
|	Quarter Rest	(an empty stem) Rest 1 beat	
⅞	Eighth Rest	Rest 1/2 beat	
▬	Half Rest	Rest 2 beats	
•	Dot	Add 1/2 value of original note	
⌒	Tie	Combines note values of two notes into one note	
0	Zero	Play string open	
2	Numeral	Number of fret to be played	
c	Choke	Left hand bends note as right hand strikes string	
s	Slide	Slide left-hand finger to sound second note	
h	Hammer-On	Add second note without restriking the string	
p	Pull-Off	Pull finger off to sound second note	
⌇ b	Brush	Strum strings so as to hear each string	

More Great Banjo Books from Centerstream...